STEALING THE LAST ARROW

The Department of Interior Indian Probate Proceedings

STEALING
THE
LAST ARROW

The Department of Interior Indian Probate Proceedings

ROBERTA CAROL HARVEY

A Citizen of The Navajo Nation

SUNSTONE
PRESS
SANTA FE

Other books by Roberta Carol Harvey from Sunstone Press:

The Earth Is Red: The Imperialism of the Doctrine of Discovery
*The Eclipse of the Sun: The Need for American Indian Curriculum in High
    Schools*
*The Iron Triangle: Business, Government, and Colonial Settlers' Dispossession
    of Indian Timberlands and Timber*
All That Glitters Is Ours: The Theft of Indian Mineral Resources
*Social Contributions of Colorado's American Indian Leaders for the Seven
    Generations to Come*
Warrior Societies A Manifesto
A Brief Colorado Indian History of 1800s, Through a Factual Lens
Indian Civics for Students
The Empty Breadbasket: The Theft of Indian Agricultural Lands

Sunstone books may be purchased for educational, business, or sales promotional use.
For information please write: Special Markets Department, Sunstone Press,
P.O. Box 2321, Santa Fe, New Mexico 87504-2321.
Printed on acid-free paper
∞
eBook: 978-1-61139-750-5

LIBRARY OF CONGRESS CATALOGING IN PUBLICATION DATA
(ON FILE)

WWW.SUNSTONEPRESS.COM
SUNSTONE PRESS / POST OFFICE BOX 2321 / SANTA FE, NM 87504-2321 /USA
(505) 988-4418

DEDICATION

With Highest Moral Obligation for Indian Allotment Owners,
Past and Present, Who Have Been Shabbily Treated

ACKNOWLEDGMENT

My Family

Nobody has been more helpful to me in the pursuit of this project than the members of my family for whom I am so very thankful. I could not have the time for research and writing without their active support. They encouraged me and made sure that whatever resources I needed for this project were available: computer, printer, supplies, etc. Thank you to my most beloved husband (who made breakfast, lunch and dinner and took over all daily family responsibilities so I could focus on this project) whose love provides such joy and stability in my life.

CONTENTS

Understaffed, Under-Funded
Lack of Functioning Communication Equipment
Hiring New Legal Assistants

Legal Defects in 2024 Individual Indian Probate Case Decision re Heirship
       Determination and Co-Owners' Option to Purchase
       Decedent's Interest in Restricted Trust Property
Dates Were Not Stated
Failure to Include Family Members of which BIA and OHA Had Been
       Given Written Notice and Confirmed as Received
Failure to Include Omitted Parties as "Interested Parties" and
       Afford Them Legal Rights
Failure to Include Co-Owners in Trust Restricted Property of which
       BIA and OHA Had Been Given Written Notice
       and Confirmed as Received
Failure to Consider Co-Owners' Option to Purchase Decedent's
       Restricted Property of which BIA and OHA Had Been Given
       Written Notice and Confirmed as Received
Failure to Conduct Formal Probate Given Restricted Trust Property Is
       Part of Decedent's Estate of which BIA and OHA Had Been
       Given Written Notice and Confirmed as Received
Failure to Give Notice to Omitted Parties of Commencement of Probate
       Proceedings in Indian Probate Case
Failure to Represent if Requisite Federal Indian Paternity Determination
       Was Made
Violation of U.S. Constitution, Statutory Law, Agency Regulations and
       Procedures, and Interior Board of Indian Appeals ("IBIA")
       Decisions
Conflicting Instructions
Petitioning for Reopening of Closed Case Is Back-End Approach
Due Process and Meaningful Opportunity to Be Heard
How to Get Notice of Federal Indian Probate Hearings
Reopening Closed Indian Probate Cases
IBIA Decisions Standard of Manifest Injustice Changed to Balancing Test
       in New Rules for Reopening Closed Indian Probate Cases
Counsel for Omitted Parties Contacted BIA and OHA Officials
       Petitioning for Reopening Indian Probate Case
Wrong Addresses on OHA Website

1: INTRODUCTION

Disclaimer

The information appearing in this book is presented for informational purposes only. The contents should not be considered as legal advice or be used as such. For legal information specific to your situation, contact appropriate legal counsel with your tribe or an attorney. Future change in laws cannot be predicted and statements in this book are based solely on the rules and regulations in force on the date of publication.

Primary Source Reliance

The author's reliance on numerous direct citations from relevant historical documents is to provide factual evidence of the subject. This format derives from her view that the material under discussion here is best experienced by the contemporaneous voice unfiltered by time or personal interpretations and revisions.

Different Names for Particular Tribes

American Indian people describe their own cultures and the places they come from in many ways. Tribes often have more than one name. When Europeans arrived in the Americas, they used inaccurate pronunciations of the tribal names or used a name that another tribe used to refer to that tribe or renamed the tribes with European names.

Different Names for Land Areas in "America"

The competition between Spain, France, Great Britain and the U.S. to establish "sovereignty" over lands inhabited by Indian peoples led to a variety of names for the same areas and 'alleged' jurisdiction over them. The U.S. would establish large Territories which would then be reduced in size to smaller territories and then become states, with modification of state lines as well.

Personal Names; Spelling

The names of historical American Indian people can cause much confusion for historians and readers. People often received several names over the course of their lives. A single person might have a birth name, a clan name, a name related to a good deed or act of bravery, and a French, Spanish, or English name used by Europeans or Americans. A tribal name could be spelled in numerous different ways.

Spelling Differed; Quotes Use Original Text

Spelling of words differed also. In this book, quotes used reflect original text, which may have different spellings, punctuation or mis-spellings or mis-punctuation. Please keep this in mind while reading this material.

"The Indian Question," General John Pope

Aaron Bird Bear explained settler colonialism to me as follows:

> Colonialism is suggested to be the policy or practice of acquiring full or partial political control over a nation, occupying it with settlers, and exploiting it economically. Additionally, settler colonialism aims for the dissolution of indigenous societies by establishing a new colonial society on seized land with the elimination of native societies as an organizing principal. Settler colonialism annihilates to supplant.

This same concept was expressed by General Pope in 1878:

> *I presume it will not be disputed that all history shows that when a savage and a civilized people are brought together in the same country, the inevitable result has been the dispossession of the savage and the occupation of the lands by civilized man.*
>
> *The first treaty made with an Indian tribe only alienated a small portion of his lands, but as the emigrants pressed forward, increasing daily both their numbers and the routes by which they entered the Indian country, it soon became necessary to make another treaty, and then another, until in time, and a very short time, as it appears, one tribe of Indians after another was dispossessed of its lands until the whole of the vast region east of the Mississippi River fell into possession of the whites.*

Accepting as inevitable the proposition that in the nature of things, the lands on this continent must in some manner and in large pass from the possession of the Indian into that of the white man ... we bought his lands by driblets, knowing very well that every purchase demanded another purchase in geometrical ratio, and that with every sale the means of livelihood upon which the Indian race had depended for ages, and which was the only mode they knew, were restricted more and more, and that in time every tribe of Indians must, in the nature of the case, be left destitute, except insofar as the government chose to feed and clothe them. The Indian did not know this in the beginning, nor indeed until want was upon him. We knew that he must relinquish in time all of his country. He did not know it, nor in the least comprehended the merciless and resistless progress of white populations. In short, we began the system, knowing perfectly what would be the results; the Indian began and for a long time continued it in ignorance of these ends.[1] (Emphasis added)

2: OFFICE OF HEARINGS AND APPEALS' ("OHA")
PROBATE PROCEDURES

Stealing Last Arrow

Peter d'Errico's phrase is poignantly fitting to the Department of the Interior's ("DOI") Office of Hearings and Appeals ("OHA") probate procedures—a **"Semantic world created by one group to rule another." Another scholar, Anthony J. Franken characterized Indian allottees in the probate arena as being 'on the whip end of someone else's crazy.'**[2] (Emphasis added) The title of Mr. Franken's article, "Dealing with the Whip End of Someone Else's Crazy: Individual-Based Approaches to Indian Land Fractionation," comes from a quote by Judge Sally Willet, explaining, the problems associated with Indian land fractionation by saying, "It is the natural consequence of congressional policies that do not take into account any practical aspects of Indian existence, ever, but think they do ... Indians are living with .. , 'the tangled effects of good and evil' or, as I say to friends, 'on the whip end of someone else's crazy.'"[3]

Bureau of Indian Affairs ("BIA") Citizenship Ceremony

The imagery of the theft of the last arrow comes from the Bureau of Indian Affairs ("BIA") Citizenship Ceremony. Individuals deemed "competent" by the BIA were encouraged to take up U.S. citizenship. The term "competent" denoted an Indian's ability to manage his/her own affairs, hold fee simple title to trust land, and be released from government control. Fee simple title is the most basic form of ownership in which the owner holds the title and total control over the property, including the right to sell, mortgage or lease.

At the ceremonial setting, a tipi was set up. The citizen-to-be was directed to enter the tipi, take off his regalia, and put on clothes a white man would wear. He was then given a white man's name, to the applause of those attending. With the Indian man properly dressed and named, the BIA representative then conducted the Ceremony:

> I hand you a bow and an arrow. Take this bow and shoot the arrow. (He shoots.) You have shot your last arrow. That means that you are no longer to live the life of an Indian. You are from this day forward to live the life of the white man. But you may keep that arrow, it will be to you a symbol of your noble race and of the pride you feel that you come from the first of all Americans.
>
> [The white name given him is now used.] Take in your hand this plow. (He takes the handles of the plow.) This act means that you have chosen to live the life of the white man—and the white man lives by work.

There was also a BIA Citizenship Ceremony for Indian women.

This photo was taken on the Standing Rock reservation during a citizenship ceremony. One man poses with a drawn bow and arrow, others hold their "last arrows." The plow and the flag are displayed as symbols of U.S. citizenship. Major McLaughlin stands at the table. Two women and one man to the right of the table appear to be wearing the citizenship badge.[4]

Office of Hearings and Appeals' ("OHA") Probate Procedures

The Office of Hearings and Appeals' ("OHA") Indian probate procedures under the American Indian Probate Reform Act ("AIPRA") steal that last arrow through equally, if not vastly more, humiliating circumstances. Indian allottees who are not lawyers try to represent themselves in proceedings before the Probate Hearings Division ("PHD") and/or the Interior Board of Indian Appeals ("IBIA"). The Decision and Orders are chock-full of legalese, intelligible to the elite cadre of over 400 licensed attorneys in the U.S. Solicitor's Office, but probably without meaning to the Indian allottees whose cases are being prosecuted. The U.S. Solicitor's Office trained corp of judges, lawyers, paralegals and legal assistants, present a formidable barrier (intended or not) for the pro se heir of an allottee. Some OHA ("PHD") Decisions or Orders, from Indian probate judges, in allotment cases may be petitioned for reopening or appealed to the IBIA, depending on the Decision and/or Order. A petition is a formal written request made to an official person or organized body such as the OHA.

> The General Allotment Act and other laws divided Indian lands among individual Indians. These separately held land parcels became known as allotments. American Indians who were originally allotted land on reservations were known as allottees. People who have inherited individual interests in allotments are typically referred to as heirs, [co-owners] or simply as landowners.[5]

> The American Indian Probate Reform Act (AIPRA) was enacted on October 27, 2004. The Act amends the Indian Land Consolidation Act (ILCA) of 1983 and ILCA amendments of 2000. Most parts of AIPRA that pertain to probate took effect on June 20, 2006. Technical amendments were signed into law December 2, 2008. AIPRA creates a uniform probate code for all reservations across the United States. The Act applies to all individually owned trust lands unless a tribe has its own probate code. All tribal probate codes pertaining to trust property must be approved by the Department of Interior. State laws no longer determine how trust lands on reservations pass from one generation to the next for individuals who pass away on or after June 20, 2006.[6]

If you pass away without writing a will, any trust or restricted land you own in the United States passes to your heirs under AIPRA. Different rules apply depending on whether you own undivided interests of less than 5% in an allotment or undivided interests of 5% or more in an allotment.[7]

The problem is even worse, according to Jared Miller, who practices Indian probate law ("Mr. Miller").

> *There is every reason to believe simple issues plague probate proceedings before they reach appeal.* That's partly because the proceedings, governed by the American Indian Probate Reform Act (AIPRA), become more complex with each new layer of regulation, including the latest one, adopted in 2022.
>
> In fact, one of the preeminent Indian probate practitioners of our time, the late Hon. James Yellowtail, in 2006 borrowed a phrase from Churchill to describe the probate process as "a riddle wrapped in a mystery inside an enigma." [He further opined that *Indian probate is "one of those cases where the imagination is baffled by the facts."*]
>
> Yet the vast majority of Native Americans represent themselves in Indian probate cases.
>
> With some estates containing big money and hundreds or thousands of acres of trust lands, it's hard to see how that reality is consistent with the federal trust responsibility owed to Indians.[8] (Emphasis added)
>
> As noted by Mr. Miller, in 2021-2022, the *IBIA docketed 31 Indian probate cases and reached the merits only four times. It dismissed most of those cases for procedural errors, like problems with service and missed deadlines, or for failure to prosecute—all problems that competent counsel could have avoided.* (Emphasis added)

The regulations themselves are very confusing. They switch back and forth between different sections of 25 Code of Federal Regulations ("CFR") and 43 CFR Parts 4 and 30. Some are only found through statutory references in the U.S. Statutes at Large, a formidable compendium indeed.

How to File an Appeal

One of the first blockades is knowing how to file an appeal.

In the *Estate of Margaret Jo Brown*, 69 IBIA 222 (12/06/2023), the petition stated: "We file a rehearing. Sincerely, Earlicia Brown". It is obvious that the individual did not know how to file an appeal. The IBIA decision stated:

> Appellant seeks review of a Notice of Filing of Petition for Rehearing by Earlicia Brown and Order Denying Rehearing (Order Denying Rehearing) entered on October 26, 2023, by Indian Probate Judge (IPJ) Thomas K. Pfister. When Appellant sought rehearing, it was her burden to allege an error of fact or law in the Decision and state specifically and concisely the grounds on which the petition was based. See 43 C.F.R. § 30.238(c). The September 18 facsimile states only: *"We file a rehearing. Sincerely, Earlicia Brown." ... The September 20 letter adds only a reference to Decedent's estate, merely stating: "We file a rehearing in Margaret [B]rown estate."* (Emphasis added)

> The IPJ denied Appellant's petition for rehearing upon finding that it failed to show proper grounds for rehearing, in that it did not allege error of fact or law in the Decision, did not state the grounds upon which it was based, and was not accompanied by any documentary evidence. Order Denying Rehearing, October 26, 2023, at 2 (citing 43 C.F.R. 30.240(c) ("If the petition fails to show proper grounds for rehearing, the judge will issue an order denying the petition for rehearing and including the reasons for denials.")

Problems with Service of Notice of Appeal

A second blockade is serving the Notice of Appeal ("NOA") on requisite parties.

> *(1) Appellant did not serve the parties listed on the distribution list; (2) under our regulations, service must be made by mail or personal delivery (and only by electronic transmission under certain circumstances that do not apply here); and (3) Appellant did not include a copy of his notice of appeal in those messages. We warned Appellant that this appeal might be dismissed without further notice if he failed to complete service, and he has not done so ...* Pre-Docketing Notice and Order for Appellant to Serve IPJ and Interested Parties. *Estate of Albert Little Owl*, 69 IBIA 338 (03/15/2024). (Emphasis added)

Serving NOA on Interested Parties Is Costly for Poor

Serving the NOA on interested parties is costly and administratively difficult. Copies of the notice of appeal, with any attachments, must be individually copied, which is costly in itself. Many appeals include numerous parties, which can easily exceed twelve. The digital divide experienced by American Indian populations is a matter of public knowledge. Many Indian families may not own a computer or printer or readily have access to a service provider such as Federal Express or UPS to make these copies.

Envelopes must be bought. They must be addressed. Postage must be secured. Mailing must be done. This is a cost in itself. To families struggling to put bread on the table, this cost is simply out of reach. To families working two or three jobs to get by, this time is not available. To disabled individuals, such as stroke victims who cannot hand-write legibly or with ease, this is not doable. To families without transportation in a rural environment, satisfying the probate procedural requirements are beyond their reach.

In an Interview with Cheryl Three Stars Valandra, Attorney, Indian Estate Planning Project of Dakota Plains Legal Services, in Mission, S.D. (Mar. 6, 2012), with Anthony J. Franken, she noted:

> … communication challenges were especially strong in poverty-stricken areas of the reservations, where three or four families may share a home and are reluctant to reveal that fact. Furthermore, many potential clients are geographically isolated, may lack telephones or even mailboxes. Elderly clients prefer face-to-face contact and some require the use of interpreters to translate the discussion.[9]

Missed Deadlines

Another blockade is missing deadlines. Indian "Appellants" have filed their NOA's with the PHD Division or the BIA Agency Superintendent, rather than mailing to the IBIA, and have missed the 30-day regulatory time period for filing appeals. It is clear they didn't know who to mail the NOA to, but in filing late, the appeal is automatically dismissed. This is repeated over and over.

> Appellant sent her letter to the Department of the Interior's Probate Hearings Division office in Billings, Montana (PHD). PHD transmitted the letter to the Board because, as provided in the Notice accompanying the Order Denying Reopening, an appeal from the order must be filed with

the Board. **We construe the letter as a notice of appeal from the Order Denying Reopening. We docket the appeal but dismiss it as untimely because the IPJ provided accurate appeal instructions, the appeal was not filed with the Board within the 30-day deadline following the IPJ's Order Denying Reopening, and the Board lacks authority to extend the time for filing a notice of appeal.** *Estate of Robert Roy Ahenakew, Jr.,* 68 IBIA 147 (04/26/2022). (Emphasis added)

Requiring NOA to Be Filed 30 Days from Date Order Was Mailed Is Unjust

Requiring a NOA to be mailed to the Board within 30 days from the date the Decision was mailed is unfair. Pro se indigent Indians in urban or rural areas may not receive a Decision requiring appeal until six or more days from it being mailed. That leaves 24 days to respond. While a NOA is a bare-bones document, it still does not mean that a pro se Appellant will even know how to respond or how to calculate the legal definition of days. Indian Probate Lawyer, Jared Miller, has offered to do this for free, knowing the poverty, lack of education, and the other circumstances prevailing in Indian communities.[10]

The terms used in these proceedings are not intelligible to pro se litigants. What is an Appellant? What is a Pre-Docketing Notice? The evidence of mailing in the *Filesteel* case is placing the items in a mailbox. It is unknown how often mail is picked up from that location or when it is date-stamped based on processing. The filing deadline was missed by one day. Pro se litigants are not going to have the money to mail documents Certified Mail, Return Receipt Requested or via a delivery service.

30 Days NOA Deadline Reminiscent of December 3, 1875, Impossible Deadline; Sioux Must Be on Reservation by January 31, 1876, or Be Attacked by U.S. Army

Sitting Bull, and many other Lakota and Cheyenne chiefs and their followers, were living outside the reservation boundaries in the Unceded Territory, still preferring to live a nomadic lifestyle predicated on bison hunting. On December 3, the Secretary of Interior sent word to the Secretary of War that he had directed the Commissioner of Indian Affairs to notify the Indians that they must move to a reservation before January 21, 1876 ("Deadline Notice") or be deemed hostile and turned over to the military force.[11]

December 20, 1875: Deadline Notice Received by Cheyenne River Agency

The deadline Notice was received by the Cheyenne River Agency on December 20, 1875. Rounding up the Lakota was a near-impossible feat in the dead of winter, yet all who refused would be considered hostile and subject to attack. Many of the Lakotas were snowbound in villages scattered throughout the Unceded Territory.[12]

December 22, 1875: Deadline Notice Received by Standing Rock Agency, Agent Requests Extension of Time due to Weather Conditions

The Commissioner's Deadline Notice was received at Standing Rock on December 22, 1875. Agent Burke requested that the Indians be given an extension of time because of weather conditions.[13]

January 31, 1876: Deadline for Sioux to Be on Their Reservation, War Declared

When January 31, 1876, arrived and only several bands of Indians had returned to the reservation, the mechanics for instituting war were set in motion.[14]

Failure to Prosecute

Many other Indian probate cases are dismissed for failure to prosecute.

> The IBIA has defined "failure to prosecute" as follows: Whenever a record discloses the failure of either party to file documents required by these rules, respond to notices or correspondence from the presiding officer, comply with orders of the presiding officer, or otherwise indicates an intention not to continue the prosecution or defense of an appeal, the presiding officer may issue an order requiring the offending party to show cause why the appeal should not be either dismissed or granted, as appropriate. If the offending party shall fail to show such cause, the presiding officer may issue an Order of Dismissal for failure to prosecute or take such other action deemed reasonable and proper under the circumstances.

Failure to Show Cause

It is unlikely an Indian Appellant would know what "show cause" means but this is another ground for dismissal. "An order to show cause (O.S.C.), is a court order or the demand of a judge requiring a party to justify or explain why the court should or should not grant a motion or a relief."[15]

Poverty Prevents Adequate Representation before IBIA

The effect of poverty in legal representation in Indian probate cases is echoed by the IBIA:

> Interested parties have a right to legal counsel, *Estate of Peahner Mahseet*, 5 IBIA 27 (1976), but **many can't afford the fees that they are required to pay because of extreme poverty in Indian country. As a result, the vast majority of heirs and beneficiaries are forced to navigate the probate process alone.** (Emphasis added)[16]

It is well-stated in Adam Crepelle's 2023 article, "Federal Policies Trap Tribes in Poverty":

> More than one in four Indians live in poverty, the highest rate of any racial group in the United States. The poverty rate is even higher for Indians who reside within Indian Country. Indian Country's poverty rate is high because there are few economic opportunities; indeed, most reservations lack any semblance of a formal, private sector. Hence, the average reservation unemployment rate has been 50 percent for decades. Due to the lack of opportunities on reservations, the median income for Indians is approximately two-thirds the median income of non-Hispanic whites.[17]

Mr. Crepelle goes on to state:

> Reservation poverty is particularly troubling given the United States has trust and treaty obligations to foster tribal economic development. Nonetheless, the United States miserably fails to allocate even basic levels of funding to tribal governments.

Indian Agent—Indian Probate Judge

David J. Wishart in his book, *An Unspeakable Sadness: The Dispossession of the Nebraska Indians*, described the Indian agent, today, in my opinion, for Indian allottees entangled in probate proceedings, replaced by the Indian Probate Judge.

> **The most powerful and pervasive intervention in Indian lives was the agent: the representative of the federal government and enactor of its policies.** Agents were charged with maintaining peace among the Indians and between Indians and Americans, with enforcing the Intercourse Laws which regulated the fur trade, with arranging for the sale of Indian lands as

needed for frontier expansion and dispensing the cash or annuities that were payments for these lands, and with promoting the civilization program. Agents varied as much in character and ability as did any other segment of American society. If the Nebraska situation can be accepted as typical, some were committed to their jobs and strove under difficult circumstances to shield the Indians from the destructive impact of the frontier; others saw the job as an easy way to earn a salary of fifteen hundred dollars a year (or more, if they embezzled), or as a convenient stepping-stone to higher office in government service. Whatever their motivations, they did little to alleviate the stress on the Indians: inefficiency was inherent in the administration of Indian affairs, programs were always inadequately funded, and in practice, if not in rhetoric, the Indians' welfare was always subordinated to the process of acquiring their lands. ... Some of the commissioners [of Indian Affairs], like Thomas McKenney (1824–30), were sincerely concerned about the fate of the Indians; others, like Elbert Herring (1831–36) and Carey Harris (1836–38), paid only lip-service to protecting their "wards" and pushed hard for the acquisition of Indian lands; all were convinced, like other Americans of the time, that the Indians had to give up their traditional lands and lifestyles, or else be crushed under the "westward march of progress." (Emphasis added)[18]

Ghost Dance

It is time to sing the prayer of the Ghost Dance: "Father, I come; Mother, I come; Brother, I come; Father, give us back our arrows."

Let us look at how we were stripped of our arrows.

Competency Commissions

In 1890, the DOI said it was the settled policy of the Government to break up reservations, destroy tribal relations, settle Indians upon their own homesteads, incorporate them into the national life, and deal with them not as nations or tribes or bands, but as individual citizens. Under the BIA Citizenship Ceremony, Indians were stripped of their Indian identity.

Representative of department speaking:

The President of the United States has sent me to speak a solemn and serious word to you, a word that means more to some of you than any other that you have ever heard. He has been told that there are some among you who should no longer be controlled by the Bureau of Indian Affairs, but should be given their patents in fee and thus become free American citizens. It is his decision that this shall be done, and that those so honored by the people of the United States shall have the meaning of this new and great privilege pointed out by symbol and by word, so that no man or woman shall not know its meaning. The President has sent me papers naming those men and women and I shall call out their names one by one, and they will come before me.

For Men:
(Read Name.)

_____ (white name). What was your Indian name? (Gives name.)

_____ (Indian name). I hand you a bow and an arrow. Take this bow and shoot the arrow. (He shoots.)

_____ (Indian name). You have shot your last arrow. That means that you are no longer to live the life of an Indian. You are from this day forward to live the life of the white man. But you may keep that arrow, it will be to you a symbol of your noble race and of the pride you feel that you come from the first of all Americans.

_____ (white name). Take in your hand this plow. (He takes the handles of the plow.) This act means that you have chosen to live the life of the white man—and the white man lives by work. From the earth we all must get our living and the earth will not yield unless man pours upon it the sweat of his brow. Only by work do we gain a right to the land or to the enjoyment of life.

_____ (white name). I give you a purse. This purse will always say to you that the money you gain from your labor must be wisely kept. The wise man saves his money so that when the sun does not smile and the grass does not grow, he will not starve.

I give into your hands the flag of your country. This is the only flag you have ever had or ever will have. It is the flag of freedom; the flag of free men, the flag of a hundred million free men and women of whom you are now one. That flag has a request to make of you, _____ (white name), that you take it into your hands and repeat these words:

"For as much as the President has said that I am worthy to be a citizen of the United States, I now promise to this flag that I will give my hands, my head, and my heart to the doing of all that will make me a true American citizen."

And now beneath this flag I place upon your breast the emblem of your citizenship. Wear this badge of honor always; and may the eagle that is on it never see you do aught of which the flag will not be proud.

(The audience rises and shouts: "_____(white name) is an American citizen.")

For Women:

_____ (white name). Take in your hand this work bag and purse. (She takes the work bag and purse.)

This means that you have chosen the life of the white woman—and the white woman loves her home. The family and the home are the foundation of our civilization. Upon the character and industry of the mother and homemaker largely depends the future of our Nation. The purse will always say to you that the money you gain from your labor must be wisely kept. The wise woman saves her money, so that when the sun does not smile and the grass does not grow, she and her children will not starve.

I give into your hands the flag of your country. This is the only flag you have ever had or ever will have. It is the flag of freedom, the flag of free men, a hundred million free men and women of whom you are now one. That flag has a request to make of you, _____ (white name), that you take it into your hands and repeat these words:

"For as much as the President has said that I am worthy to be a citizen of the United States, I now promise to this flag that I will give my hands, my head, and my heart to the doing of all that will make me a true American citizen."

And now beneath this flag I place upon your breast the emblem of your citizenship. Wear this badge of honor always, and may the eagle that is on it never see you do aught of which the flag will not be proud.

(The audience rises and shouts: "_____(white name) is an American citizen.")[19]

1922: Hidatsa Chief Old Dog

When citizenship was offered Hidatsa Chief Old Dog in 1922, he declined. "I do not want the white man's offer of citizenship. I have lived a long life, and I have seen many of the Great White Fathers' promises vanish on the winds. I do not need the white man's government to tell me that I am free."[20]

Dispossessing Indians of Land and Resources

Dispossessing Indians of their land and resources followed a common trajectory.

It started with the legal fiction that Indians didn't own their land, but were mere tenants at sufferance, permitting their ouster from their land. If they were tenants, they didn't own the natural resources on their lands.

The tactics to accomplish this dispossession included intimidation, lying, stealing, cheating, harassing, trespassing, fraud, mispresenting the value of Indian land and resources, removal, extermination, massacres, private wars funded by the federal government, war crimes, massive cession of lands, concentration and consolidation of Indians on reservations, allotment of tribal land to individuals to break up the tribal mass, alienability of allotments and termination. Repudiating the sovereignty of Indian nations and assimilating Indians into the body politic wasn't questioned. These practices were endorsed by the President, the executive branch, the military, Congress and the judiciary. With this impetus, states selected their own method for securing for their citizens the inexhaustible mineral, agricultural, water and natural resources within their dominion. Big business used its political and economic clout to assure its imperial control of the country's natural wealth. Settlers were the boots-on-the-ground.

3: TREATY ERA

Treaties are legally binding agreements between two or more sovereign governments. Treaties with Indian nations were negotiated and concluded by a representative of the President and became binding agreements after they were ratified by a two-thirds majority vote of the U.S. Senate.

In numerous treaty conferences held between the highest-level of Crown and colonial officials and Indian leaders, Indian nations were considered the sovereign owners of their land. The credibility of the sovereignty of the Indian tribes was recognized by Justice Story. He was an American lawyer, jurist, and politician who served as an associate justice of the Supreme Court of the United States from 1812 to 1845. He is remembered for his Commentaries on the Constitution of the United States, first published in 1833.

> § 3. There is no doubt, that the Indian tribes, inhabiting this continent at the time of its discovery, maintained a claim to the exclusive possession and occupancy of the territory within their respective limits, as sovereigns and absolute proprietors of the soil. They acknowledged no obedience, or allegiance, or subordination to any foreign sovereign whatsoever; and as far as they have possessed the means, they have ever since asserted this plenary right of dominion, and yielded it up only when lost by the superior force of conquest, or transferred by a voluntary cession.[21]

There are 389 treaties with Indian nations. With the end of treaty making in 1871, the federal government continued to enter into similar legal relationships with tribes under statutes, executive orders, and other agreements such as Presidential proclamations.

Act to Regulate Trade and Intercourse with Indian Tribes

In 1790, Congress adopted the Act to Regulate Trade and Intercourse with the Indian Tribes, the first of several such acts specifically governing commerce with

Indian nations and travel by non-Indians onto Indian land. The Act established the federal government's preemptive right to purchase Indian lands, excluding states or other entities from the right to negotiate to purchase land. Indian nations maintained title to and exclusive jurisdiction over their lands, but they could not sell land to whomever they wished.

American Land Policy

American land policy, from the start, was designed to bolster the settlement and creation of permanent non-Indian family-sized farms, without any regard for Indian rights.

By allowing generous credit terms in spreading out payments for land over four years, purchasing land became more feasible. *This policy choice by the U.S. served the purpose of getting the land promptly settled in the Ohio River Valley and the Great Lakes, both as a buffer against British aggression.*

To make Indian land theft even easier, the Land Act of 1800 gave settlers the right to purchase the land on which they squatted at the minimum price. Their chronic indebtedness and lack of hard cash, along with the popular belief that the squatters were doing a national service by clearing the land and extending the area of civilization, led to rewarding them for their illegal squatting. Few farmers could raise $640 to buy a wilderness farm site, even with four years to pay.

The Land Act abolished the credit system but it revised purchase regulations to make it possible for anyone with $100 to buy an 80-acre tract. The price was still beyond the reach of thousands of debt-ridden farmers, so they simply squatted where they chose without title to the land.[22]

Military Warrants or Scrip

About 73.5 million acres of federal land nationwide were disbursed under military land bounties and warrants to veterans. Military warrants gave 160 acres of free land to every enlisted man who served at least five years. Initially, the land had to be within a federal military reserve and the warrants were nontransferable—other requirements were designed to encourage veterans to settle along the "Indian frontier."

Originally, only the land and not the scrip could be transferred, but in 1852 Congress made the scrip transferable.[23] In Minnesota in the 1850s, for example, lumber companies obtained much of the forest land in the St. Croix Triangle by buying military warrants from veterans. Land in northern Minnesota was similarly purchased with military warrants. Many veterans sold their warrants to land speculators, timber companies, and others, for as little as 10 cents an acre, not knowing or caring about the value of the land and instead seeking the immediate cash.[24]

European Investment Aided in Indian Land Dispossession

European capital was highly sought after by U.S. land speculators and investors who sent influential Americans abroad to generate interest. As François Furstenberg notes in his probing analysis of the role of European capital in frontier America:

> ... the funneling of European capital into the northern and northwestern [American] backcountry may well be one of the most important - and most overlooked - features of the post-Revolutionary era. ... It was European capital, not American, that began to integrate the northern U.S. backcountry into the Atlantic world's trade networks.[25]

Executive Conflict of Interest

The president's conflict of interest between the trust responsibilities to Indians and the obligations to the citizenry started early on. By 1821, their policies of removal, cession of lands, and allotment of tribal land to individuals were voiced well in advance of any legislation.

President John Adams: Indian Trust Responsibilities Are Subordinate to Obligations to U.S. Citizenry

President John Adams (1797-1801) captured the essence well of the executive responsibility to its "white children" in this 1878 letter to the Cherokee Nation objecting to the invasion of squatters:

His "stronger obligations" were to "hear the complaints, and relieve, as far as in my power, the distresses of my white children, citizens of the United States."[26] These 'white children' had the right to vote, an important consideration for any elected official.

President Thomas Jefferson: Architect of Indian Removal

Thomas Jefferson (1801–1805) would become the (1) architect of the U.S.' Indian removal policy, well before the Indian Removal Act of 1830; and (2) the "Manifest Destiny" of the U.S. to expropriate Indian lands.

From Thomas Jefferson to John Breckinridge (U.S. Attorney General), 12 August 1803, regarding the Louisiana Purchase:

> … the best use we can make of the country for some time will be to give establishments in it to the Indians on the East side of the Mispi in exchange for their present country, and open land offices in the last, & thus make this acquisition the means of filling up the Eastern side instead of drawing off its population. when we shall be full on this side, we may lay off a range of states on the Western bank from the head to the mouth, & so range after range, advancing compactly as we multiply.[27]

His ideology of expansionism was voiced in 1780 when he coined the phrase "Empire of Liberty," while the American Revolution was still being fought. In his instructions to George Rogers Clark to take Fort Detroit he envisioned a future of commerce and expansion:

> We shall divert through our own Country a branch of commerce which the European States have thought worthy of the most important struggles and sacrifices and … shall form to the American union a barrier against the dangerous extension of the British Province of Canada and add to the Empire of Liberty an extensive and fertile Country …[28]

President James Madison: Severalty Policy Is Precursor to Allotment

The fourth President, James Madison, planned to complete the work of transitioning the Indians from the "habits of the savage to the arts and comforts of social life" and divide up their land in a terrifying precursor to future allotment. By the political administration of Indians in reduced areas, land expropriation and exploitation would be easier.

> [T]he facility is increasing for extending that divided and individual ownership, which exists now in movable property only, to the soil itself, and of thus establishing in the culture and improvement of it the true foundation for a transit from the habits of the savage to the arts and comforts of social life.[29]

President James Monroe: Extinguishment of Indian Title Inevitable; Removal of Indians Paramount; Assimilation Policy Defunct

The fifth President, James Monroe, in his First Annual Message to Congress proclaimed his success in extinguishing Indian title in seven states: Ohio, Michigan,

Indiana, Georgia, North Carolina, Tennessee and Alabama and pursuing his goal also of individual allotted Indian ownership of land.

> From several of the Indian tribes inhabiting the country bordering on Lake Erie purchases have been made of lands on conditions very favorable to the United States, and, as it is presumed, not less so to the tribes themselves.

> In this progress, which the rights of nature demand and nothing can prevent, marking a growth rapid and gigantic, it is our duty to make new efforts for the preservation, improvement, and civilization of the native inhabitants. The hunter state can exist only in the vast uncultivated desert. It yields to the more dense and compact form and thus was given to mankind to support the greatest number of which it is capable, and no tribe or people have a right to withhold from the wants of others more than is necessary for their own support and comfort.

> It is gratifying to know that the reservations of land made by the treaties with the tribes on Lake Erie were *made with a view to individual ownership among them* and to the cultivation of the soil by all, and that an annual stipend has been pledged to supply their other wants. (Emphasis added) A considerable and rapid augmentation in the value of all the public lands, proceeding from these and other obvious cases, may henceforth be expected.[30]

Second Inaugural Address of James Monroe, March 5, 1821

> The care of the Indian tribes ... has not been executed in a manner to accomplish all the objects intended by it. We have treated them as independent nations, without their having any substantial pretensions to that rank. The distinction has flattered their pride, retarded their improvement, and in many instances paved the way to their destruction. The progress of our settlements westward, supported as they are by a dense population, has constantly driven them back, with almost the total sacrifice of the lands which they have been compelled to abandon. Their sovereignty over vast territories should cease, in lieu of which the right of soil should be secured to each individual and his posterity in competent portions.[31]

Five weeks before President Monroe left office, he declared that the removal of the Indians was of paramount importance to the U.S. The concept of assimilation was officially defunct. In 1825, ominously, he acknowledged that without protection, they were doomed to extermination.

"Experience has clearly demonstrated that in their present state it is impossible to incorporate them in such masses, in any form whatsoever, into our system," Monroe stated. "It has also demonstrated with equal certainty that without a timely anticipation of and provision against the dangers to which they are exposed, under causes which it will be difficult, if not impossible, to control, their degradation and extermination will be inevitable."[32]

The Monroe administration would eventually conclude a total of forty-one treaties with twenty-nine different Indian nations. All but eight involved a cession of Indian lands to the U.S.

Of the eight remaining treaties, in accord with Secretary of War Calhoun's policies, six placed the signatory Indian nations under the protection, and de facto sovereignty, of the U.S. For Calhoun, anything short of "a complete extension of the laws and authority of the U.S. over the Indians was unacceptable." Any Indian authority was to be choked off.[33]

In proclaiming the Monroe Doctrine of 1823, President Monroe adopted an isolationist policy, which advocates minimal participation of a country in the internal affairs of another nation, and, an interventionist policy, which believed that prohibiting certain forms of intervention or involvement are necessary to protect economic and political national interests. Thus, anyone seeking to colonize the Americas would face the utmost resistance. The doctrine proposed the following key elements: The American continents should not be considered for future colonization by the European powers; any attempt by European countries to impose their system on any nation in the western hemisphere would be considered by the U.S. to be a threat to their own peace and safety; and the U.S. in turn would not interfere in European affairs. President Monroe knew that building empires involves not just acquiring new land or territories, but also exercising political economic, and military control over other nations.

1823: U.S. Supreme Court Chief Justice Marshall's Epithet of Indians' Savagery

The usual practice of assimilating conquered people as citizens of the conquering government was not possible with 'fierce savages,' according to the U.S. Supreme Court Chief Justice John Marshall in his decision in *Johnson v. M'Intosh*, 21 U.S. 543, 590 (1823):

But the tribes of Indians inhabiting this country were fierce savages, whose occupation was war, and whose subsistence was drawn chiefly from the forest. To leave them in possession of their country was to leave the country a wilderness; to govern them as a distinct people was impossible, because they were as brave and as high spirited as they were fierce, and were ready to repel by arms every attempt on their independence.

Marshall Trilogy

Three cases: M'Intosh, Cherokee Nation and Worcester represent the Marshall Trilogy and fundamentally shaped federal Indian policy and institutionalized major doctrines of federal Indian law: Johnson v. M'Intosh, 21 U.S. 543 (1823); *Cherokee Nation v. Georgia*, 30 U.S. 1 (1831); and *Worcester v. Georgia*, 31 U.S. 515 (1832). The Trilogy, primarily authored by Chief Justice John Marshall, established federal primacy in Indian affairs, excluded state law from Indian Country, and recognized tribal governance authority.

M'Intosh incorporated the Doctrine of Discovery into federal law. Under the Doctrine of Discovery whichever European nation first 'discovered' land, then not ruled by a Christian prince or people, could claim ownership of the land as against other European nations, even if it was inhabited. The discovering Christian country acquired the 'fee simple absolute' title to the land, which is a term meaning the unlimited ownership interest in the land. Indians only had the right to occupy the land; they didn't own it. Their 'right of occupancy' could be purchased or won by conquest.

Cherokee Nation characterized tribes as 'domestic dependent nations,' not foreign nations. Indian tribes were understood to be wards of the federal government. The federal government was authorized to make decisions for the Indians.

Worcester held that state law does not apply in Indian Country. This was recently modified by a majority of the U.S. Supreme Court in 2022 in the case, *Oklahoma v. Castro-Huerta*. Under this case, the federal government and the state have concurrent jurisdiction to prosecute crimes committed by non-Indians against Indians in Indian Country.

Congress Has Plenary Authority over Indian Nations

In the case of *Lone Wolf v. Hitchcock*, 187 U.S. 553 (1903), the Supreme Court announced that Congress had plenary authority over Indian nations. It can limit tribal powers, enhance them by delegating new powers to tribes, or even terminate tribal status. Congress' power comes from authority delegated to Congress by the Indian Commerce Clause of the U.S. Constitution. Pursuant to this plenary authority, Congress may unilaterally break treaties with the Indian nations in order to allot their reservations and give the land away to non-Indians. Indian nations do not have recourse to the federal courts to remedy violations of treaties by the federal government.

Power of Congress over Indian Affairs May Be Plenary, But It Is Not Absolute

In *Delaware Tribal Business Committee v. Weeks*, 430 U.S. 73 (1977), the Court held that "The power of Congress over Indian affairs may be of a plenary nature; but it is not absolute." Federal legislation must be rationally related to furtherance of the federal trust responsibility to Indians. However, rational basis scrutiny is not a strong standard for review of Congressional action.

4: REMOVAL ERA

In 1817, in a letter to John Adams, General Jackson refused to recognize Indian nations as sovereign. Jackson declared, "I have long viewed treaties with the Indians an absurdity not to be reconciled to the principles of our Government." The Indians, said Jackson, were subjects of the U.S., pure and simple, "inhabiting its territory and acknowledging its sovereignty." It was a fiction that the tribes were in fact separate and independent entities, and it was absurd to negotiate with them as such.[34]

1824: Secretary of War Threatens Cherokees: They Will Be Left to Whims of Georgia

In 1824, Secretary of War John Calhoun threatened to leave the Cherokees "exposed to the discontent of Georgia and the pressure of her citizens" if they continued to refuse to exchange their land in Georgia for land west of the Mississippi. They responded: "Sir, to these remarks we beg leave to observe, and to remind you, that the Cherokees are not foreigners, but original inhabitants of America; and that they now inhabit and stand on the soil of their own territory; and that the limits of their territory are defined by the treaties which they have made with the Government of the United States."[35]

Secretary of War James Barbour's February 1826 plan for the Indians made it clear that, in the eyes of the government, the Indians must be removed—but not, as had often been promised in earlier years, for the benefit of being free from settler corruption and abuse but to destroy their autonomy. This seeming federal support led the Georgians to vigorously pursue inclusion of Indian land under state hegemony.[36]

1827: Conflict between Creek Indians and State of Georgia Leads to Federal Threat of U.S. War against State

In 1827, President John Quincy Adams, sent a message to Congress which he termed "most momentous." He informed Congress that the Creeks had invoked the protection of the federal government to defend their rights as guaranteed by a ratified treaty. "Their forbearance and reliance on the good faith of the United States will, it is hoped, avert scenes of violence and blood, which there is otherwise too much cause to apprehend." The message then delineated the stipulations of the Trade and Intercourse Act of March 30, 1802, and the punishments prescribed for colonial settler intruders in Indian Country. There was no previous instance in which the disagreement between state and federal authority had been "urged into a conflict of actual force"—if not civil war, at least a potential prelude to it.[37]

President Adams warned Georgia:

> ... it is my duty to say, that if the legislative and executive authorities of the State of Georgia shall persevere in acts of encroachment upon the territories secured by a solemn treaty to the Indians, and the laws of the Union remain unaltered, a superadded obligation, even higher than that of human authority, will compel the Executive of the United States to enforce the laws, and fulfill the duties of the nation by all the force committed for that purpose to his charge.[38]

The Adams administrations' saber rattling to protect the rights of the Creek Indians and Georgia's Governor to prevent precisely that meant that the potential for armed collision between different branches of the federal system fizzled, with the Adams' administration unwillingness to go to war. A select Senate committee chaired by the powerful Senator Thomas Hart Benton requested the President to take every action possible to convince the Creeks to accept payment for their lands. Benton included a dire warning.

> "The committee will not enlarge upon the frightful consequence of civil wars," he wrote. "They are known to be calamitous to single Governments, and fatal to confederacies. A contagious fury rages in such contests. No matter how small the beginning, or how insignificant the cause, the dissension spreads, until the whole confederacy is involved."[39]

Negotiations commenced that summer with the Creeks, before Congress even approved funding for a cession of Indian lands, which allowed for a cooling off period. In the autumn, the Creeks ceded their lands.

1828: Removal Supported by Eastern and Christian Groups and U.S.

Removal was also supported by many Eastern and Christian groups who regularly expressed sympathy for American Indians. Thus, in 1828, U.S. Indian Commissioner Thomas McKenney wrote, "What are humanity and justice in reference to this unfortunate race?"[40]

The solution lay in geography—place Indians so far west that colonist settlement would not be a problem for a very long time, perhaps centuries. The federal government should create "a land of refuge, where this unhappy race may find rest and safety," wrote Lewis Cass, shortly before he became Andrew Jackson's Secretary of War.[41]

1828: Andrew Jackson's Indian Removal Presidential Campaign

Andrew Jackson's Presidential Campaign in 1828 made American Indian Removal his goal—relocating eastern Indians west of the Mississippi River.

> As cotton culture spread across Georgia, federal officials proved either unwilling or unable to extinguish quickly enough for land-hungry Georgians the claims of the Creeks and the Cherokees to lands within the state. Angered over the delay in fulfilling the terms of the Compact of 1802, Georgia's leaders, throughout the 1820s and 1830s, regularly prodded the President then in office to complete the process of Indian removal. In 1820, a congressman from Georgia bitterly complained that when the state gave up its claim to western lands to the federal government in 1802, everyone assumed they would quickly gain title to the land from Indians and open it to settlement. Many Georgians were concerned that many Indian nations, particularly the Creek and the Cherokee, were not interested in selling land, much less leaving. What the Georgians refused to acknowledge was that 90 percent of Indian land claims within the state had been extinguished, at enormous cost, instead accusing the federal government of bad faith and threats of armed conflict.[42]

Just nineteen days into his presidency, in a bold move, Jackson stated his removal policy in a speech to the Creek Indians.

> Where you now are, you and my white children are too near to each other to live in harmony and peace. Your game is destroyed and many of your people will not work and till the Earth. Beyond the great river Mississippi, where part of your nation has gone, your father has provided a country

large enough for all of you, and he advises you to remove to it. There your white brothers will not trouble you; they will have no claim to the land, and you can live upon it, you and your children, as long as the grass grows or the water runs, in peace and plenty. It will be yours forever.[43]

THE Creek Indians informed the federal government that, "We deem it impolitic and contrary to the true interests of this nation to dispose of any more of our country." The commissioners sent by Washington, D.C., offered a chilling reply: "If you wish to quit the chase, to free yourself of barbarism, and settle down in the calm pursuits of civilization, and good morals, and to raise up a generation of Christians, you had better go." If you choose otherwise, "You must be sensible that it will be impossible for you to remain for any length of time in your present situation as a distinct Society or Nations, within the limits of Georgia. Such a community is incompatible with our System and must yield to it."[44] THE continuing tension between Indian nations and states is but the continuing issue of an 'imperium in imperio.' No state wants another state within its boundaries.

1829: Georgia Enacts Laws Abolishing Cherokee Indian Sovereignty, Self-Government and Right to Land

THE state of Georgia enacted laws abolishing the Cherokee's right to sovereignty, self-government and land. President Jackson and Congress refused the direct request of the Cherokee Nation for federal intervention to uphold their Hopewell Treaty (1785) rights against Georgia's legislative encroachments.

Georgia's first act was passed December 12, 1829, and is entitled:

> An act to add the territory lying within the chartered limits of Georgia, and now in the occupancy of the Cherokee Indians, to the counties of Carroll, De Kalb, Gwinnett and Habersham, and to extend the laws of the State over the same, and to annul all laws made by the Cherokee Nation of Indians ... Resolved, Indians are tenants at her will, and that she may at any time she pleases, determine that tenancy, by taking possession of the premises.[45]

1829: Gold Discovered on Cherokee Lands

When gold was discovered on Cherokee land, the state of Georgia passed another act, entitled "An act to authorize the Governor to take possession of the gold, silver, and other mines lying and being in that section of the chartered limits of Georgia commonly called the Cherokee country, and those upon all other unappropriated lands of the State, and for punishing any person or persons who may hereafter be found trespassing upon the mines."

In 1829, Hezekiah Niles, editor of the Niles Weekly Register newspaper, offered the starkest comment on removal: "The fate of the Indians within the present states and territories—is sealed." The eastern Indian nations would move or become extinct.[46]

1829: If Congress Rejects Cherokee Petition and Georgia's Laws Are Enforced, Cherokee Will Be Removed Without Difficulty

Arguments that the Indians would move if Congress did not respond favorably to their petitions to remain in the southeast were discussed by high-ranking military officials who recommended rejection of their petitions:

> In 1829, General Carroll described the difficulties he met with in inducing the Indians to emigrate to the secretary of war: "The truth is, they rely with great confidence on a favorable report on the petition they have before Congress. If that is rejected, and the laws of the States are enforced, you will have no difficulty of procuring an exchange of lands with them."

> General Coffee, upon the same subject says, "They express a confident hope that Congress will interpose its power, and prevent the States from extending their laws over them. Should they be disappointed in this, I hazard little in saying that the government will have little difficulty in removing them west of the Mississippi."[47]

Exterminate, Assimilate, Protect or Remove Indians

Four alternatives identified with regard to Indians included: exterminating them, assimilating them, protecting them or removing them. Exterminating them was not realistic. The U.S. Army was small, with only seven infantry regiments responsible for manning forty-nine military posts and arsenals from Maine to Florida and from Louisiana to Michigan. War would be too costly in money and American lives. Assimilation was considered impractical. Affording meaningful protection was impossible, militarily and, even more importantly, politically. The government lacked the finances and the U.S. Army lacked the will to fend off the squatting colonists. Removal, sanctioned from President Jefferson to Jackson, represented the only viable action. With the defeat of such renowned Indian leaders, as Pontiac, Tecumseh, Little Turtle, Blue Jacket, McGillivray, John Ross and Black Hawk, there remained no effective Indian resistance.

In 1829, the support of the New York Indian Board, long an advocate for Indians, agreed that removal was the only viable alternative:

> … the harmony of these United States, the preservation of the American Indians from total extinction, and consequently the cause of humanity, require some prompt and decisive measure calculated to carry into effect the only alternative left, namely, the final and speedy removal of the scattered remains of the Indian tribes from within the jurisdictional limits of the sovereign states.[48]

1830: Andrew Jackson's Justification for Indian Removal

In 1830, President Jackson justified Indian removal based on his beliefs that the Indians were savages and had made no improvements to the U.S.:

> What good man would prefer a country covered with forests and ranged by a few thousand savages to our extensive Republic, studded with cities, towns, and prosperous farms, embellished with all the improvements which art can devise or industry execute, occupied by more than 12,000,000 happy people, and filled with all the blessings of liberty, civilization, and religion?[49]

1830: Tenor of Times: They May Begin to Dig Their Graves and Prepare to Die

In 1830, Alfred Balch, Jackson's Commissioner of Indian Treaties, echoed the tenor of the times: "…removal of Indians would be an act of seeming violence — But it will prove in the end an act of enlarged philanthropy. These untutored sons of the Forest, cannot exist in a state of Independence, in the vicinity of the white man. If they will persist in remaining where they are, they may begin to dig their graves and prepare to die."[50]

1830: Indian Removal Bill Introduced in Congress

Jackson's Commissioner of Indian Treaties Balch's assurance to Jackson that he would ramrod Indian removal legislation through Congress was underway. On February 24, 1830, Tennessee Rep. John Bell and the Indian Affairs committee introduced a removal bill—officially, H.R. 287. The Senate version of the bill, submitted at the same time by Bell's counterpart on the Senate's Indian Affairs committee, Hugh Lawson White, was known as S. 102.[51]

The House version of the bill was preceded by a report of over 15,000 words that was part opposition to removal, part history of U.S. Indian policy, especially the peculiarities of the treaty system, and part assertion of the southern Indians' rapid decline and, should they remain, certain extinction.

The introduction of the Indian Removal Bill led to lengthy debates in the public and in Congress. President Jackson emphasized that the emigration of the Indians "should be voluntary, for it would be as cruel as unjust to compel the aborigines to abandon the graves of their fathers and seek home in a distant land."[52] In support of Georgia, those Indians who remained would be subject to the authority of local and state law and jurisdiction.

Reports from Indians that had moved west, however, were dismal and the southern Indians feared for their survival. In 1826, General Clark, Superintendent of Indian Affairs, credits the southern Indians fear of moving with the dire stories of the Indians who had moved west.

> The condition of many tribes west of the Mississippi is the most pitiable that can be imagined. During several seasons in every year, they are distressed by famine, in which many die for want of food, and during which the living child is often buried with the dead mother, because no one can spare it as much food as would sustain it through its helpless infancy.[53]

1830: Congressional Senate Debates on Indian Removal Act Challenging 'Doctrine of Discovery' and Occupancy Indian Land Tenure Theory

The Congressional Senate debate on the Indian Removal Act lasted from April 6 to April 24, 1830. Of the 48 senators, only eight spoke for any length of time—four of whom voted for the removal bill, four against. Senator Theodore Frelinghuysen of New Jersey and his allies, Peleg Sprague of Maine and Asher Robbins of Rhode Island, intended to prove that the Act violated the higher authority of the U.S. as expressed in its treaties with the Indians. Opposing them were John Forsyth of Georgia, Hugh Lawson White of Tennessee, John McKinley of Alabama and Robert Adams of Mississippi.

1830: Georgia's Governor Gilmer Eviscerates Treaties between U.S. and Indians

Georgia Governor Gilmer averred on the Congressional floor that Indian treaties were meaningless:

> ...treaties were expedients by which ignorant, intractable, and savage people were induced without bloodshed to yield up what civilized peoples had a right to possess by virtue of that command of the Creator delivered to man upon his formation-be fruitful, multiply, and replenish the earth, and subdue it.[54]

Also, he remarked "I will have my bond, I will have my pound of flesh," declaring that he would have the terms of the Compact of 1802 fulfilled to "the twentieth part of one poor scruple, and to the division of a hair." Under the Compact of 1802, Georgia gave up claims to western lands and in exchange the federal government agreed to extinguish the Cherokee Indian land title and remove the Cherokees from the state.

Speech of Senator Frelinghuysen of New Jersey: Indians Held Original and Absolute Title to Their Lands

Senator Theodore Frelinghuysen from New Jersey, in his six-hour speech opposing the Indian Removal Act, asserted three fundamental and, as he saw it, undeniable precepts about the relationship of the Indians to the U.S.:

(1) the Indians held the original and absolute title to their lands - *"I insist that, by immemorial possession, as the original tenants of the soil, they hold a title beyond and superior to the British Crown and her colonies, and to all adverse pretensions of our confederation and subsequent Union. ... Where is the decree or ordinance that has stripped these early and first lords of the soil? Sir, no record of such measure can be found."*

(2) the Indian tribes were sovereign political entities with their own governments - Our ancestors found these people, far removed from the commotions of Europe, exercising all the rights, and enjoying the privileges of free and independent sovereigns of this new world. *They were not a wild and lawless horde of banditti; but lived under the restraints of Government, patriarchal in its influence.—They had chiefs, head men and councils* ...[55] (Emphasis added)

Importantly, Senator Frelinghuysen emphasized that grants to the King, Colony, State or Territory of Indian lands were made from the Indians, not from the governing authority to them:

> No King, Colony, State or Territory, ever made, or attempted to make, a grant or title to the Indians, but universally and perpetually derived their titles *from* them. This one fact, that stands forth broadly on the page of Indian history-which neither kings nor colonies-neither lords, proprietors, nor diplomatic agents, have on any single occasion disputed, is alone sufficient to demolish the whole system of political pretensions, conjured up in modern times to drive the poor Indian from the last refuge of his hopes.[56]

He refused to concede that the citizens of the new republic would agree to the false front Georgia was using to take away the lands of the Cherokees. There were many who stood with him in speaking the truth, but unfortunately, not enough.

> *The people of this country will never acquiesce in such violent constructions. They will read for themselves; and when they shall learn the history of all our intercourse with the Indians; when they shall perceive the guaranties so often renewed to them, and under what solemn sanctions, the American community will not seek the aids of artificial speculations on the requisite formalities to a technical treaty. No, Sir.*[57] (Emphasis added)

He also condemned the 'most odious proposal' to divide, conquer and bribe Cherokee leaders and influential men. In the instructions of the Secretary of War to Gens. Carroll and Coffee, is found the following language: "The best resort [to induce the Indians to emigrate] is believed to be that which is embraced in an appeal to the chiefs and influential men-*not together, but apart at their own houses-* and be a proper exposition of their real condition, rouse them to think upon that; whilst *offers to them of extensive reservations in fee simple,* and *other rewards,* would it is hoped, result in obtaining their acquiescence."[58]

William Lloyd Garrison would later compose a poem honoring Senator Frelinghuysen and assailing the motives of the Act's supporters.

TO THE HON. THEODORE FRELINGHUYSEN: ON READING HIS ELOQUENT SPEECH IN DEFENCE OF INDIAN RIGHTS, IN THE UNITED STATES SENATE

> Fruitless thy mighty efforts—vain appealing
> To grasping Avarice, that ne'er relents;
> To Party Power, that shamelessly is stealing,
>
> Banditti-like, whatever spoil it scents;
> To base Intrigue, his cloven foot revealing,
> That struts in Honesty's habiliments.

Speech of Senator Sprague of Maine: Cherokees Promised Undisturbed Possession of Their Land

Senator Sprague of Maine focused on the fourteen treaties entered into with the Cherokees promising them protected, undisturbed possession of their lands. He vigorously contested Georgia's assertions that the treaties were informal, and hence malleable. He then went on to enunciate the obligations under these treaties.

> By several of these treaties, we have unequivocally guaranteed to them that they shall forever enjoy—
>
> 1st. Their separate existence as a political community;
> 2d. Undisturbed possession and full enjoyment of their lands, within certain boundaries, which are fully defined and fully described;
> 3. The protection of the United States, against all interference with, or encroachments upon their rights by any people, state, or nation. For these promises, on our part, we received ample consideration. By the restoration and establishing of peace; By large cessions of territory; By the promise on their part to treat with no other state or nation, and other important stipulations.
>
> Did this give to the United States the right to drive them from all their lands?—Or to destroy the Cherokee Nation, to strike it out of existence; and instead of managing for their 'benefit' to annihilate 'their affairs' as a body politic?[59]

Speech of Senator Robbins of Rhode Island: Indians Victims of Violated Justice

> The whole argument in favor of this bill turns upon the question, whether the Indian nations within our territorial boundaries are competent to make treaties with the United States. I should think, to make gentlemen

pause a little, and even fear the success of their own argument; for the consequence would be such that the whole body of the rights acquired by Indian treaties or held under them, would be torn from their foundations, and the resulting evils would be incalculably great.

I will say, that these Indians have been made the victims of power exerted against right; the victims of violated faith, the nation's faith; the victims of violated justice; yes, I call God to witness of his violated justice.

Ill fated Indians! barbarism, and attempts at civilization, are alike fate to your rights; but attempts at civilization the more fatal of the two. The jealous of their own rights are the contemners of yours; proud and chivalrous states do not think it beneath them to take advantage of your weakness. You have lands which they want or rather which they desire … Proud and chivalrous states do not think it beneath them to present to your feeble and helpless condition, this alternative-either to abandon your homes, the habitations you have built, the fields you have planted, and all the comforts you have gathered around you; the homes of your fathers, and the sepulchers of their dead; and go far into the depths of an unknown wilderness; there to abide the destiny which may there await you; or to surrender your rights, and submit yourselves to their power, but to expect no participation in their rights.[60]

Georgia's legislation was yet another tactic of settler colonial policy—get Indians to voluntarily move, rather than endure living under the cloak of tyranny. Also, the various removals of different Indian nations caused a dispersal of Indians and a weakening of their status as sovereigns.

Congressional House of Representatives Debates on Indian Removal Act Challenging 'Doctrine of Discovery' and Occupancy Indian Land Tenure Theory

Other opponents of the Indian removal legislation in the House of Representatives similarly agreed with Senator Frelinghuysen, including Henry Storrs of New York, William Ellsworth and Jabez Huntington of Connecticut, George Evans of Maine, Isaac Bates and Edward Everett of Massachusetts, John Test of Indiana, Jensey Johns, Jr., of Delaware, David Crockett of Kentucky and Joseph Hemphill of Pennsylvania. They labelled removal plans as open and rank assaults on Indian sovereignty. Prominent members of Congress characterized the bill as designed to flout firm and binding treaty obligations. They also assailed the provisions of the removal bill itself, arguing that it was vague in its goals and unrealistic in its expectations.

Speech of Representative Storrs: Georgia's Debt Made Her Situation Precarious; Needed Cherokee Land

Representative Henry Storrs in his speech reveals the major problem at hand for Georgia—her citizens didn't have the money to pay taxes and her debt made her situation precarious.

> I have been inclined to think, Sir, that under all the circumstances, some of the new states were admitted into the Union before they had acquired a sufficient population and strength to sustain their State ...[61]

Rep. Storrs, also, denounced the bribery proposed by Jackson's Secretary of War Eaton: "It is sheer, open bribery — a disreputable proposition to buy up the chiefs, and reward them for treason to their people."

Representative Storrs was also opposed to portraying treaties as other than a negotiated agreement between sovereigns:

> The committee [on Indian Affairs] have suggested that we should not give much weight to 'the stately forms which Indian treaties have assumed, nor to the terms often employed in them,' but that we should rather consider them as 'mere names' and 'forms of intercourse.' If treating these Indian nations as proprietors of a qualified interest in the soil - as competent to enter into treaties - to contract alliance - to make war and peace - to stipulate on points involving and often qualifying the sovereignty of both parties, and possessed generally of political attributes unknown to individuals, and altogether absurd in their application to subjects, is nothing more than 'mere names' and 'stately forms,' then this long practice of the Crown, Colonies, the States, and the Federal Government, indeed, proves nothing. **Words no longer mean what words import, and things are not what they are.** (Emphasis added)[62]

In addition, he raised the critical question of conquest. If the U.S. was to argue it conquered the Indians, where were the attributes of conquest?

> But it is essential to title by conquest, that we should have exercised the right which the laws of war allow to the conqueror. **Have we taken away their lands, abolished their governments, and put them in subjection to our laws.** ... So far from claiming to exercise this right, we have closed our hostilities by treaties ever since we became an independent government ... (Emphasis added)[63]

Speeches of Other Advocates for Indian Rights: "I Fear, with Self-Reproach, Regret as Bitter as Unavailing"

Should the members of Congress sanction removal, said Rep. Woods, "the blood of these People, reduced by us to the condition of wretchedness and horror, in which 'the living child is buried with the dead mother,' will be upon our heads."[64]

Representative Isaac Bates of Massachusetts accused Jackson and his supporters of bad faith even more pointedly. "You cooperate with Georgia—you give effect to her laws—you put the Indians aside and trample your treaties with them in the dust," Bates alleged. "And it will be in vain you tell the world you did not set fire to the city, when you saw it burning, and would not put it out, though you were its hired patrol and watch."[65]

Representative Edward Everett, Massachusetts, decried it as follows:

> The evil, Sir, is enormous; the inevitable suffering incalculable. Do not stain the fair fame of the country.... And we ourselves, Sir, when the interests and passions of the day are past, shall look back upon it, I fear, with self-reproach, and a regret as bitter as unavailing.[66]

Representative David Crockett, Kentucky, represented more citizens than any other representative. He voted with his conscience against removal.

> He knew the Indians were unwilling to go and therefore he could not consent to place them in a situation where they would be obliged to go. ... He knew that he stood alone, having, perhaps, none of his colleagues from his state agreeing in sentiment. ... Humble as he was, he meant to exercise his privilege.[67]

Memorial of Cherokee Nation (April 14, 1830)

When the Cherokee Nation petitioned Congress to prohibit Georgia's incursion on its lands, they confirmed the government's recognition of their ownership of their land:

> It is evident from facts deducible from known history, that the Indians were found here by the white man, in the enjoyment of plenty and peace, and all the rights of soil and domain, inherited from their ancestors from time immemorial, well furnished with kings, chiefs, and warriors, the bulwarks of liberty, and the pride of their race. Great Britain established with them

relationships of friendship and alliance, and at no time did she treat them as subjects, and as tenants at will, to her power. In war she fought them as a separate people, and they resisted her as a nation. In peace, she spoke the language of friendship, and they replied in the voice of independence, and frequently assisted her as allies, at their choice to fight her enemies in their own way and discipline, subject to the control of their own chiefs, and unaccountable to European officers and military law. Such was the connexion of this nation to Great Britain, to wit, that of friendship, and not allegiance, to the period of the declaration of Independence by the United States.[68]

1830: Indian Removal Act Passed

In 1830, Congress passed the act titled: "An Act to provide for an exchange of lands with the Indians residing in any of the states or territories, and for their removal west of the river Mississippi," commonly referred to as the Indian Removal Act of 1830, 4 Stat. 411. It passed the Senate by a vote of 28-19. It passed the House by a vote of 102-97. It was signed by President Andrew Jackson on May 28, 1830. It included funds to pay for removal—$500,000 was appropriated to pay to move Indians west of the Mississippi River. The bill, conspicuously, contained no stipulation which allowed the Indian nations to refuse relocation or even any indication they might not wish to do so, and nothing further was said of assimilation. It made no mention of the use of force.

Three days later the House also passed the Preemption Act of 1830, giving squatters a right of first refusal to purchase land they had occupied prior to its being opened for sale.

More distressing was the policy to use the squatters as 'hired guns,' a military force against the Indians. They were willing to vigorously protect their alleged land rights. "*Settlers presented the Indians with a large local militia that made the odds of a victorious attack so low that, realizing their weakness, the tribes sold out cheaply. However, opposed the common law tradition might be to squatters, these settlers played an important role in expropriating Indian lands at minimal cost.*" (Emphasis added) Kades, Eric. "The Dark Side of Efficiency: Johnson v. M'Intosh and the Expropriation of American Indian Lands." *University of Pennsylvania Law Review* (2000).

Removal of Indian Nations Became Mandatory

Over 60 removal treaties were signed which resulted in the forced westward migration of approximately 80,000 American Indians. Although removal was supposed to be voluntary, relocation of Indian nations became mandatory whenever the government decided. Many of the eastern Indian nations were destroyed or decimated. Millions of acres of lands were opened to settlers.

Other Southern States Follow Georgia's Lead

The states of Alabama (Creek Indian Nation), Mississippi (Chickasaw and Choctaw Indian Nations) and Tennessee (Cherokee Indian Nation) also enacted laws that abolished the Indian nations rights to sovereignty and land.

Removal of 'Five Civilized Tribes' Accomplished

The Choctaw were removed in 1831 (Treaty of Dancing Rabbit Creek). The Seminole were removed in 1832 (Treaty of Payne's Landing). The Creek were removed in 1834 (Treaty of Washington). The Chickasaw were removed in 1837 (Treaty of Pontotoc). The Cherokee were removed in 1838 (Treaty of New Echota, 1833).

Alexis de Tocqueville, French Diplomat, Political Scientist and Historian, Author of *Democracy in America*, Witnessed Removal of Choctaws

At the end of the year 1831, while I was on the left bank of the Mississippi, at a place named by Europeans Memphis, there arrived a numerous band of Choctaws... These savages had left their country and were endeavoring to gain the right bank of the Mississippi, where they hoped to find an asylum that had been promised them by the American government. It was then the middle of winter, and the cold was unusually severe; the snow had frozen hard upon the ground, and the river was drifting huge masses of ice. The Indians had their families with them, and they brought in their train the wounded and the sick, with children newly born and old men upon the verge of death.

They possessed neither tents nor wagons, but only their arms and some provisions. I saw them embark to pass the mighty river, and never will that solemn spectacle fade from my remembrance. No cry, no sob, was heard among the assembled crowd; all were silent. Their calamities were of ancient date, and they knew them to be irremediable. The Indians had all stepped into the boat that was to carry them across, but their dogs remained upon the bank.

As soon as these animals perceived that their masters were finally leaving the shore, they set up a dismal howl and, plunging all together into the icy waters of the Mississippi, swam after the boat.[69]

5: Reservation Era

The 1851 Indian Appropriations Act allotted funds to move western tribes onto reservations. The BIA defines a reservation as "an area of land reserved for a tribe or tribes under treaty or other agreement with the United States, executive order, or federal statute or administrative action as permanent tribal homelands, and where the federal government holds title to the land in trust on behalf of the tribe."[70]

> In the first announcement made of the reservation system, it was expressly declared that the Indians should be made as comfortable on, and as uncomfortable off, their reservations as it was in the power of the Government to make them; that such of them as went right should be protected and fed, and such as went wrong should be harassed and scourged without intermission.[71]

Commissioner N.G. Taylor expressed the government's position on the need to dispossess Indians of the abundant and valuable natural resources on their aboriginal homelands. In 1868 he stated as follows:

> The steady approach of emigration ... imperiously demand that the policy of concentrating them upon reservations should, whenever practicable, be adopted. ... The Indians are in possession of vast tracts of country, abounding in precious metals, or rich in sources of agricultural wealth. These invite the enterprise of the adventurous pioneer, who, in seeking a home and fortune, is constantly pressing upon the abode of the red man.[72]

1862: Inadequate Appropriations

The inadequate appropriations by Congress for food, clothing and other needs of Indians resulted in some of the bleak stories of man's inhumanity. Indian men, women and children, unable to meet their most basic needs, died from starvation and exposure.[73]

Commissioner Morgan in 1890 in hindsight reflected on the infinite horror of the reservation system:

> The entire system of dealing with them is vicious, involving, as it does, the installing of agents, with semi-despotic power over ignorant, superstitious, and helpless subjects; the keeping of thousands of them on reservations practically as prisoners, isolated from civilized life and dominated by fear and force; the issue of rations and annuities, which inevitably tends to breed pauperism; the disbursement of millions of dollars' worth of supplies by contract, which invites fraud; the maintenance of a system of licensed trade, which stimulates cupidity and extortion, etc.[74]

Failure to Fulfill Trust Responsibilities

Maura Grogan in her article, "Native American Lands and Natural Resource Development," Revenue Watch Institute, identifies three components of the federal trust responsibility: "the protection of Indian trust lands and Indian rights to use those lands; the protection of tribal sovereignty and rights of self-governance; and the provision of basic social, medical and educational service for tribal members."[75]

In 1869 President Grant appointed a commission composed of "nine men, representing the influence and philanthropy of six leading States, to visit the different Indian reservations, and to `examine all matters appertaining to Indian affairs.'" Their report includes the following language:

> While it cannot be denied that the government of the United States, in the general terms and temper of its legislation, has evinced a desire to deal generously with the Indians, it must be admitted that the actual treatment they have received has been unjust and iniquitous beyond the power of words to express. … *The history of the government connections with the Indians is a shameful record of broken treaties and unfulfilled promises. The history of the border white man's connection with the Indians is a sickening record of murder, outrage, robbery, and wrongs committed by the former as the rule*, and occasional savage outbreaks and unspeakably barbarous deeds of retaliation by the latter as the exception.
>
> *In addition to the class of robbers and outlaws who find impunity in their nefarious pursuits upon the frontiers, there is a large class of professedly reputable men who use every means in their power to bring on Indian wars, for the sake of the profit to be realized from the presence*

of troops and the expenditure of government funds in their midst. They proclaim death to the Indians at all times, in words and publications, making no distinction between the innocent and the guilty. They incite the lowest class of men to the perpetration of the darkest deeds against their victims, and, as judges and jurymen, shield them from the justice due to their crimes. Every crime committed by a white man against an Indian is concealed or palliated ...[76] (Emphasis added)*

Clearly, the federal government was failing in its trust responsibilities to Indians.

Savage Aristocracy

Negative, demeaning stereotypes were used to justify taking Indian lands:

> It has seemed to me ... that the system of large reservations as has hitherto prevailed, is not only no longer desirable either in the interest of the Indians or of the whites, but will, in the course of time become utterly untenable. As our white settlements in the West multiply, as the development of the country advances, available lands become more and more scarce and valuable, and so it is not unnatural that the withholding of large tracts from settlement and development so as to maintain a savage aristocracy in the enjoyment of their chivalrous pastimes, should be looked upon by many as a system incompatible with the progress of civilization and injurious to the material interests of the country. As an inevitable consequence, we have witnessed many encroachments, lawless and wrongful in character, upon Indian lands and rights, and constant efforts to drive the red men from the reservation belonging to them.

> ... as long as the Indians hold very large tracts of land, in great part useless to themselves ... their tenure will, under existing circumstances become practically more and more precarious. It is most desirable for the interests of the Indians themselves, therefore, that we should substitute for the system of large reservations another system that will protect the rights and interests of the Indians without standing in the way of the progress and development of the country. The ultimate end of this new system, in my opinion, must necessarily be that the Indians be gradually assimilated to and merged in the body of citizens. In the direction of this end, some things are necessary, which have been done as far as the Executive could do them under the laws of the country as they stand: First, to set the Indians to work; second, to educate them; and, third, to individualize the Indians by settling them in severalty, with the expectation of giving them fee-simple

title by patent to their allotments, the same title by which white citizens hold their lands under the protection of law.[77]

1871: Treaty-Making with Indian Nations Abolished

Formal treaty making ended when Congress, with a rider in the Appropriation Act of March 3, 1871 (16 Stat. 544, 25 U.S.C. 71), prohibited the federal government from making new treaties with American Indian tribes. The text reads: "No Indian nation or tribe within the territory of the United States shall be acknowledged or recognized as an independent nation, tribe, or power with whom the United States may contract by treaty; but no obligation of any treaty lawfully made and ratified with any such Indian nation or tribe prior to March 3, 1871, shall be hereby invalidated or impaired..."

6: ALLOTMENT ERA

The Allotment Era resulted in Indian Country's most significant loss of land after reservations had already been established—90 million acres were alienated.

1876: Commissioner Smith Advocates Allotment

Commissioner of Indian Affairs Smith, in 1876, put the burden on Indians to adapt to agricultural lifestyles and become self-supporting, notwithstanding that "the adventurous, grasping Anglo-Saxon race is dominant and in possession of the fairest and richest portions of the land." He pronounced that:

> "The next twenty-five years are to determine the fate of a race. If they cannot be taught, and taught very soon to accept the necessity of the situation and begin in earnest to provide for their own wants by labor in civilized pursuits they are destined to speedy extinction. ..." He recommended: First. Concentration of all Indians on a few reservations. Second. Allotment to them of lands in severalty. Third. Extension over them of United States law and the jurisdiction of United States courts.[78]

1878: "Outrageous Frauds" Committed at Isabella Reservation, Michigan, on Land Patented in Fee to Indians

The effect of allotment was a period of fraud and calumny.

An investigation by Special Agent Edwin Brooks in 1878 at the Isabella Reservation uncovered "outrageous frauds." He was called back to Washington on his arrival at the Reservation but stayed an extra day to complete his brief investigation due to the extent of the frauds he uncovered. His handwritten Report is 38 pages long (names are redacted herein). He urged that the DOI consider criminal prosecution, finding in particular that in issuing 1,735 patents at Isabella, Indian Agent George Betts had deemed a mere 24 allottees as "not so competent" to receive their patents in fee.[79]

Competency was described as follows: "Those who are intelligent and have sufficient education and are qualified by business habits to prudently manage their own affairs." [p. 10].

Agent Brooks described the land as follows: "large quantities of it was very valuable pine, and the remainder among the finest agricultural land in the State" [p. 12].

> At the time the selections were made, there was a great struggle on the part of various speculators and lumbermen to obtain title to the lands selected. Prior to the making of the lists, these parties had, by competent agents, been over the whole reservation and estimated the timber on the tracts. When the lands were selected and before the lists were approved or patents issued deeds to the timber on large quantities of the pine lands were taken by various parties among them ... and for a large portion of which but a mere tithe of the actual value of the timber was paid. [pp. 12-13] ...

> [O]f the records of Isabella County ... have 822 deeds for timber purchased from Indians on record and up to the present time they have recorded in said records 855 deeds... [pp. 14-15]. __ has title to, I think, at least one hundred selections ... and a pretended receipt taken which was in fact a Warranty Deed. [p. 16].

> I saw at least a hundred Indians ... listed as competent, not one of whom was, in my judgment, in any way capable of transacting any kind of business. [p. 18].

> ... such wholesale frauds could not have been conceived and executed without the connivance of the agents. [p. 20].

> These facts, if no others existed, are sufficient to show fraud and collusion of the darkest character on one side, and on the part of the Indians, a degree of ignorance and incompetency alone sufficient to warrant the office in cancelling the whole list. [p. 25].

> The facts discovered by the brief investigation made, in my opinion, conclusively show that the schedule ... is in the main fraudulent, that it was prepared by an Agent in collusion with, and in the interest of a pack of unscrupulous land sharks seeking and conspiring to defraud the Government and the Indians of a large tract of valuable land... [pp. 34-35].

The parties ... are wealthy and more than ordinarily influential in civil, religious and political circles, and will doubtless suppress an investigation ... [p. 37].

Eventually a government investigation forced the Isabella Reservation Indian Agent to resign, but not before five-sixths of the land he had allocated to Saginaw-Chippewa Tribal members had been sold. [p.19] In all, about 75,000 acres were sold, of which the federal government eventually returned 6,500 acres to reserve land status.

1878: DOI Had Complete Knowledge of Frauds at Isabella Reservation

If there is any doubt that the DOI had complete knowledge of the frauds committed at the Isabella Reservation, one need only read the written statement by Commissioner Ezra A. Hayt detailing the frauds. This statement documents the absolute and total failure of the DOI to protect Indian lands on the Isabella Reservation.

But after the issue of patents, the difficulties surrounding them do not cease. A few, it is true, hold to their land and make rapid and encouraging progress in agricultural pursuits. The major portion of them, however, yielding to the pressure surrounding them, fall victims to the greed of unscrupulous white men, and, one by one, part with or are defrauded of their lands. Every means that human ingenuity can devise, legal or illegal, has been resorted to for the purpose of obtaining possession of Indian lands.

In some cases title in severalty in fee simple has been given to the individual members of the tribes for a certain quantity of the land embraced in the reservation.

Experience has shown that even the most advanced and civilized of our Indians are not capable of defending their lands when title in fee is once vested in them. The reservations in such cases are at once infested by a class of land-sharks who do not hesitate to resort to any measure, however iniquitous, to defraud the Indians of their lands. Whiskey is given them, and while they are under its influence they are made to sign deeds of conveyance, without consideration. They are often induced to sign what they are informed is a contract of sale for a few trees growing on their land, with a receipt for the consideration paid; or some party goes to them claiming to be an agent of the State or county, distributing funds to the poor. This party will pay the Indian five or ten dollars, and procure his signature to a pretended receipt for the same, when in reality the paper signed is a warranty deed, which is recorded, and generally the land is sold to a third and innocent party before the Indian discovers the fraud which has been practiced upon him.

In other cases the Indians complain, and, as it appears, not without cause, that they are subjected to unequal and unjust taxation which they are unable to meet, and are thus divested of the title to their lands.

Again they are induced to mortgage their lands for small sums which they are told will enable them to make money and improve their farms as their white neighbors have done. These mortgages are small payable generally at a time when the Indians are likely to have no money; an attorney fee of seventy-five or one hundred dollars is inserted. At maturity if the mortgage is not satisfied, which generally happens, foreclosure is had, the land is sold, and the Indian is left homeless and hopeless, a pauper for the community to support.

Out of 1,735 Indians to whom patents were issued about the year 1871 on the Chippewa Reservation of Isabella County, Michigan, fully five-sixths have sold, or in some manner have been cheated out of their land.[80]

1887: General Allotment Act

The General Allotment Act ("GAA") or Dawes Act of 1887, divided Indian tribal land into individual allotments, forcing Indians into private property ownership. Up until this time the reservations had been held communally by all members of the tribe(s) living on the reservation. The alleged rationale for the GAA was that it would assimilate Indians into the mainstream of U.S. society by encouraging farming and agriculture. Also, a transition to farming would lessen the amount of land needed by Indians such that it would justify reducing their land base. Alternatively, there was no need for a separate land base for Indians assimilated into the general society.

To that end, individual Indians were given a certain number of acres, generally in 40-, 80- and 160-acre parcels, to be held in trust by the U.S. for the individual for 25 years and then patented in fee.[81] Allotment was not new; certain treaties provided for it prior to the GAA, but the GAA enshrined it into law.

After the twenty-five years that the allotment was held in trust by the U.S., it was expected that the Indian owner would be "civilized" and "competent enough" to manage his own affairs and the government would issue a fee patent for his allotment. (General Allotment Act § 5). The term "patent-in-fee" describes the title document issued by the U.S. to terminate the trust created by the trust patent issued to the allottee. The patent-in-fee operates to vest fee simple ownership in an allottee or their heirs.

Reservation lands not allotted or reserved for tribal or other use were considered surplus to Indian needs and opened to purchase and settlement by non-Indians. While the GAA marked the destruction of a tribe's land base, the Burke Act of 1906 triggered the rapid loss of lands from individual Indian ownership. The Burke Act amended the GAA by authorizing the secretary to issue a patent in fee on allotments before the expiration of the twenty-five-year trust period "whenever he shall be satisfied that any Indian allottee is competent and capable of managing his or her affairs".[82] Once an individual was certified competent, the Burke Act authorized the issuance of a fee patent to the allottee, immediately subjecting his/her lands to state property taxes and the option of sale to Indians or non-Indians.[83]

Commissioner of Indian Affairs Atkins would expound from the bully pulpit:

> The advantages to the Indians of taking their lands in severalty are so important and far-reaching in their effects that I fear to dwell upon them in this report …Every step taken, every move made, every suggestion offered, everything done with reference to the Indians should be with a view of impressing upon them that this is the policy which has been permanently decided upon by the Government in reference to their management. They must abandon tribal relations; they must give up their superstitions; they must forsake their savage habits and learn the arts of civilization; they must learn to labor, and must learn to rear their families as white people do, and to know more of their obligations to the Government and to society. In a word, they must learn to work for a living, and they must understand that it is their interest and duty to send their children to school.[84]

Colorado Senator Henry Teller tried, unsuccessfully, to change the Republican Party policy on Indian Affairs. In 1881, when allotment was being studied, he said that the policy would "despoil the Indians of their lands and make them vagabonds on the face of the earth."

> The Minority Report of the House Indian Affairs Committee stated: that "the real aim [of allotment] was to get at the Indian lands and open them up to settlement. The provisions for the apparent benefit of the Indians are but the pretext to get at his [the Indians'] lands and occupy them... If this

were done in the name of greed it would be bad enough; but to do it in the name of Humanity, and under the cloak of an ardent desire to promote the Indian's welfare by making him like ourselves, whether he will or not, is infinitely worse."[85]

Congress Enacts Major Crimes Act, GAA and Opens Unassigned Lands to White Settlement

During President Cleveland's first term in office, from 1885 to 1889, Congress enacted three measures with devastating effects on Indians. First, the Major Crimes Act (18 U.S.C.S. §1153) instituted federal jurisdiction over serious crimes committed by Indians on their own land. This deprived Indian nations of this vital aspect of sovereignty, especially since the federal government lacked the manpower and the will to prevent criminal activities. Second, the GAA (25 U.S.C.S. §§331 et seq.) authorized the President to divide Indian tribal land into individual allotments, forcing Indians into private property ownership whether they desired it or not. Third, the Indian Appropriations Act of 1889 (c. 412, 25 Stat. 980) opened "unassigned" lands to white settlers. This would lead, for example, to the Oklahoma Land Run of 1889.

1889: Nelson Act

In 1889, Minnesota Representative Nelson introduced an act for the "relief and civilization of the Chippewa Indians in the State of Minnesota." Congress passed the 'Nelson Act' on January 14, 1889. It implemented, in Minnesota, the applicable provisions of the GAA. It instructed the President to negotiate with *all of the Chippewa Indians in the State of Minnesota for the complete cession of all of their title and interest to all of the reservations in the State, except the White Earth and Red Lake Reservations.* (25 Stat. 642). (Emphasis added)

White Earth and Red Lake Reservations, Minnesota

The lands at White Earth and Red Lake Reservations in Minnesota were to be allotted, with the surplus left over after allotment to the Chippewas to be offered for sale and opened to white settlement. Lands classified as agricultural lands were to be disposed of at a $1.25/acre under the Homestead Act. Section 3 of the Nelson Act provided an exception to removal to White Earth for those Indians who took an allotment on their existing reservation. This exception resulted in many Indians taking an allotment on their reservations, defeating the consolidation of Chippewas at White Earth.

Red Lake Reservation, Minnesota

The minutes of the negotiations by the Rice Commission, appointed to negotiate with both the Red Lake and the White Earth Bands of the Chippewa Indians for cession and relinquishment of certain lands, show that the Commission assured the Chippewas on the Red Lake Reservation that the land which it would reserve out of their reservation after allotment would belong to them and their children; that enough land would be reserved for them and their descendants for all purposes; that no other Indians would have any right therein; and that no allotments would be made immediately out of the land reserved. The Band was at all times steadfastly opposed to allotment of the 661,118 acres it reserved.

May-Dway-Gon-On-Ind, head chief of the Red Lake Band, stated: "I will never consent to the allotment plan. I wish to lay out a reservation here, where we can remain with our bands forever. I mean to stand fast to this my decision, whenever the Government feels inclined to pay for the lands."[86] He further stated: "We want the reservation we now select to last ourselves and our children forever. I shall touch the pen with the understanding that all you have said to us is the truth; that you respect the truth and the words of our Great Father."[87]

A letter from Commissioner E. M. Browning to the Secretary of Interior, dated May 9, 1896, stated in part:

> As I have said, I doubt the expediency of making allotments in severalty to the Red Lake Indians ... it was plainly and unmistakably their understanding, in signing the agreement that they were not to take their allotments in severalty; and this opposition has continued and still exists. Should the Department at this time attempt to force allotments upon them, the Commission would doubtless meet with strong and almost irresistible opposition.[88]

> The Secretary of Interior responded in part on August 4, 1896: "Concurring in your views, as to the matter of allotments to the Red Lake Indians and for the reasons stated by you, you are directed to instruct the Chippewa Commission to take no steps to make allotments to the Red Lake Band of Chippewas at present."[89]

The Red Lake Reservation was therefore not allotted, even though mandated by the Nelson Act.

Adult Mixed-Bloods Free to Sell Their Land

The Steenerson Act of 1904, authored by Minnesota Rep. Halvor Steenerson, doubled the size of allotments from 80 to 160 acres. Minnesota Senator Moses Clapp's rider on the 1904 Indian Appropriations Act, introduced one day after the Steenerson Act, removed the restriction prohibiting adult "mixed-blood" Indians from selling their allotments prior to the expiration of the twenty-five year trust period. They did not have to wait before receiving a fee patent. They were free to sell their lands. The Clapp Rider further allowed full-bloods to apply for the removal of restrictions on the sale of their allotments, if the DOI determined he/she was competent of managing his/her affairs.

White Earth Reservation, Minnesota: How to Steal Indian Lands

In 1905, the White Earth Reservation, comprising 750,000 acres in northwestern Minnesota, belonged to the Chippewa Indians residing there, either as individual allottees or as property held in trust for them by the federal government. The land was physically varied with good soil for farming; plentiful timber; and amidst the lakes and streams, hunting, fishing and wild rice for harvesting. Railroad lines ran near the Reservation's northern and southern boundaries and along its western edge.

The lumber industry had harvested the southern timber in Minnesota. It needed to move north in search of more pine to feed the state's mills—three out of four were the world's largest. More were springing up. The combination of logging companies, bankers, mortgage companies, wealthy investors and attorneys stood to make a bundle of cash from the timber located on Indian lands.

Stage Was Set to 'Get Rich Quick' Off of White Earth Indian Lands

Anthropologist Warren Moorehead's first-person account discloses the confederation behind the scenes to 'get rich quick' off of Indian timber and arable land:

> The effect of the allotment on the Whites near White Earth was immediate. Mushroom banks sprang up in the surrounding small towns. The Indians in their affidavits (of which Linnen and myself took 505) testified that lawyers, banks, county officials, and business men of prominence in Detroit, Ogema, Mahnomen, and other towns, joined in the scramble to secure their pine lands and farm tracts... in the majority of cases, as the Indian could neither write nor read, he did not know whether he was signing receipts, mortgages, deeds or releases.[90]

In tandem with Moorehead, contemporary historian William Folwell reported:

> Purchases from adult mixed-bloods might be strictly legal, even though they were not equitable; but fullbloods and minors were not legally competent to sell. In utter violation of law, land sharks from near and far bought allotments of full-bloods and took their deeds and had them recorded. … Some operators did not scruple to obtain conveyances from minors … Ignorant Indians were fleeced.[91]

Cat's Out of the Bag

On July 18, 1906, a Minneapolis newspaper reported that land speculators were plying the Indians with liquor in order to secure deeds or mortgages to their lands for small amounts; that the town had been filled with drunken Indians; and that 250 allotment mortgages had been filed at Detroit and many more in Norman County.

1909: Commissioner Valentine: Get to Bottom of Thieving at White Earth

Indian Commissioner R.G. Valentine ordered an investigation. Fully ninety per cent of the allotments to full-bloods had been sold or mortgaged and *eighty per cent of the whole acreage of the reservation had passed into private hands*. Full-bloods had received not more than ten per cent of the value of their land and timber. (Emphasis added)[92]

The reports of trickery, deception and fraud were substantiated by the DOI in its investigation in 1910.

> The allottees began to sell their lands as soon as the act was passed. The cupidity of the white purchasers led to flagrant violations of the law. They purchased lands of Indians who were unquestionably full-bloods and plainly not competent to sell their lands under the law. Trickery and fraud of all kinds was resorted to, and finally about 95 per cent of the allotments, or the timber on the allotments, of White Earth allottees had been disposed of under the pretended authority of the law mentioned. Millions of dollars were involved in these illegal sales. DOI needs to get lands back.

In 1911, the Commissioner of Indian Affairs further reported:

> It was early discovered that there existed hundreds of fraudulent conveyances of both land and timber of full-blood and minor Indians, and the question

of protecting the interests of these Indians by actions in the courts was, as soon as the facts could be obtained, referred to the Department of Justice.[93]

Complete success means the recovery of 142,000 acres, valued at over $2,000,000, and for timber valued at $1,755,000, on behalf of more than 1,700 Indians, forming almost 34 per cent of the White Earth allottees.[94]

Ransom Powell Ransomed His Timber Company Clients

The timber industry retained attorney Ransom Powell. *First*, he used the easiest and strongest defense of all: delay. Documents get lost; memories fade; witnesses can't be located; government attorneys turn over frequently versus having an attorney handling one issue for the long run; and parties give up. *Second*, he needed to establish mixed blood status since (a) they had the right to sell their allotments; and (b) they presented the majority of the cases. *Third*, knowing that most Indians didn't have the money to bring a case, he pursued a novel theory: the federal government didn't have the right to represent individual Indian defendants since they had a state court forum for their fraud cases and he won the case he filed.

U.S. Proves Criminal Conspiracy in Full-Blood Quantum Case

In the meantime, an early prosecution of a full-blood case was successful for the government and the Indians. Banker and developer M. J. Kolb and J.E. Perrault were found guilty of "criminal conspiracy and inducing federal officials to issue land patents to full blood Indians." They were given modest fines, but no criminal sentence or record. The defendants made restitution in money and restored title amounting to approximately $10,000. Thirteen Ojibwe whose lands had already been transferred by Kolb were awarded amounts ranging from $400 to $1,400 which were escrowed with the Agency Superintendent. Ojibwe lands still in the defendants' possession were restored to trust status.[95]

Quantum of Blood of Ojibwes Determined by Comparing Them to "Pure" Southwestern Pima Indians

In 1914 with timber-company funds, Powell hired two anthropologists for the identification of Ojibwe full-bloods and mixed-bloods. Dr. Albert E. Jenks, a professor at the University of Minnesota, and Dr. Ales Hrdlicka examined 696 Ojibwe who claimed to be full bloods, comparing their physical attributes to the Pima Indians of the southwestern U.S., whom the anthropologists considered the most racially "pure" American Indians. They carefully measured and calibrated hair, eyes, nails, gums, head shapes, and teeth of White Earth Ojibwe and compared this data to measurements of the Pima.[96]

Their studies narrowed the pool of full-bloods. *Of the 5,173 White Earth allottees, only 408 were considered to be full bloods - and 306 of them died before the roll was finalized in 1920.* Based on the government studies, in 1920, there were only *102 full-blood White Earth Ojibwes.* The results of this study still stand today given Judge Page Morris, Senior Judge of the United States District Court for the District of Minnesota, approving the roll and placing it on file with the Clerk of Court in Fergus Falls, Minnesota. In *Bisek v. Bellanger*, 5 F.2d 994, 995 (D. Minn. 1925), the "Blood Roll" was upheld.

Government's White Earth Cases Weakened by Powell's Advocacy

Due to Powell's *first defense*—delay—he won. The DOJ determined that it would be difficult to successfully prevail at trial given the *decade* that had passed since starting the litigation. They agreed on a settlement basis:

The 2,000 suits filed by the federal government involving over 2,500 allotments and 142,000 acres of land, asserting that White Earth allotments had been fraudulently obtained from full-bloods and minors would be settled. Land would be restored to full bloods; the cases involving mixed bloods who were competent to sell would be dismissed; and others who were defrauded, such as minors, would receive the difference between their original payments and the fair value of the property at time of sale, plus six percent interest to the time of settlement [not their land]. Significantly, no remedy was established for mixed bloods who had been defrauded.[97]

Powell ensured that most of his clients' purchases were protected for a comparatively small cost. Nichols-Chisholm paid only $48,497 and its sister firm, Park Rapids Lumber, only $23,015.[98]

Allotment of Indian Lands in Utah No Different

Arthur Lloyd Thomas was appointed as Governor of Utah in 1889 by Pres. Harrison. He requested the early allotment of Uintah Reservation lands.

> Much land within these reservations is useless for either cultivation or grazing, while some of it is of immeasurable value for mining. ... When such circumstances are combined, the effect of the reservation is clearly that of restriction of the best interests of the Territory and its people, and

without any advantage to anyone else. *The early adoption of an Indian policy which will abolish the tribal organization of the Indians, and give them in severalty whatever land they can use, will be worth millions of dollars to the people of the Territory.* (Emphasis added)[99]

In 1893, he reported that the Uintah Reservation lands are:

> ... some of *the most fertile and well-watered lands within the Commonwealth.* As the acreage per capita for the Indians is so unnecessarily large as to be entirely beyond reason, I have to recommend that *early provision be made for the allotment in severalty* of suitable quantities of such land to the Indians, and that the remainder of the lands be then thrown *open to the public for settlement.* (Emphasis added)[100]

1894: Utah's Legislative Push for Opening Both Uintah and Ouray Reservations

Utah's territorial delegate to Congress, Joseph L. Rawlins, sponsored a bill in 1894 to *open both the Uintah and Ouray Reservations in eastern Utah to white settlement.* Under provisions of his bill, certain land within the reservation would be given in severalty to the resident Utes, and the rest of the land would then be sold in lots not exceeding 160 acres to whoever submitted the highest sealed bid.

Utah's Governor West continued his advocacy for opening the Reservations:

> The Congressional legislation authorizing the allotment to the Indians, in severalty, of certain of the lands embraced within the Uintah and Uncompaghre reservations and the opening for settlement and sale of the remaining lands, as recommended by me in my last report, will prove of untold advantage and wealth to the new State. *It will open for settlement millions of acres of the most fertile and perfectly watered lands, and will furnish homes for thousands* of our young people who need no longer emigrate to the valleys of adjoining States for suitable locations. The undeveloped mineral resources will undoubtedly attract much attention, and, together with the magnificent opportunities afforded the home seeker of the already overcrowded East, will be the means of causing a material increase in our population and taxable wealth. (Emphasis added)[101]

> Under the State government we confidently anticipate an influx of population sufficient to strengthen our cities, cultivate our valleys, and *as soon as the Indian reservations are thrown open for settlement, to*

completely transform them into productive gardens and fields, thrifty villages and towns. (Emphasis added)[102]

Land Tenure on Allotted Reservations

The Native Lands Advocacy Project explains the key problems of fractionation and checkerboarding as follows.

a) Fractionation: A fractionated land title is one where multiple individuals own a single parcel of land. The number of owners can increase exponentially with each generation to the hundreds or thousands. Most of these owners must agree to any land use decision. This often prevents any Indian landowners from benefitting from their land.

b) Checkerboarding: The pattern of adjoining land parcels with different types of ownership is known as checkerboarding. Reservations often include segments of individual trust land, tribal trust land, non-native fee land, federal, state and municipal land. [The pattern of mixed ownership resembles a checkerboard.] These fall under different jurisdictions, causing Indian nations difficulty in asserting regulatory and legal control and fostering development. Checkerboarding can also simply physically prevent access to Indian lands.[103]

In 1935, an Indian Land Tenure, Economic Status, and Population Trends Report on Land Planning was issued ("Land Planning Report"). The BIA contribution to the Report documents the devastation of allotment on Indian lands, lives and communities.

As the Indians disposed of their allotments, a steady stream of whites filtered into every corner of the reservation. The connecting tissue of white social and economic life rapidly overshadowed that of the Indians. Indian fashion, the landless and homeless ex-allottees domiciled themselves with their relatives, thus overpopulating the remaining Indian lands and pressing upon their subsistence capability. Today practically every map of an allotted reservation which shows the present ownership of land, both Indian and white, resembles the face of a checkerboard. *Thus, while the white newcomers steadily consolidated their holdings into good, usable farming and grazing units through their purchases from the allottees, supplemented by leasing, exactly the opposite effect was being worked upon the lands remaining in Indian ownership.* (Emphasis added)[104]

Inadequate Capital and Lack of Agricultural Equipment and Education

As reported by the BIA, in the years following the passage of the GAA, tribal lands were allotted to individuals who were then expected to farm successfully without training, tools, or equipment.

> In 1888 Congress appropriated $30,000 for seed, farming implements, and other things necessary for farming. *In that year there were 3,568 allotments, so that the fund provided an average of less than $10 to each allottee. In 1889 Congress again appropriated $30,000. In the following year nothing was appropriated; but in 1891, 1892, and 1894, annual appropriations of $15,000 were made. Thereafter until 1911, nothing was appropriated.* That year Congress established a loan fund. Approximately $250,000, or about $1.50 per capita of the Indian population, has been annually set aside for this purpose - a woefully inadequate amount to help the Indians to their feet. A total of about $5,000,000 has been loaned from this source, of which $2,000,000 has been repaid by the Indians. ... (Emphasis added)[105]

> Practical assistance to the Indians was limited to the appointment of Government "farmers" and "stockmen." As is well known, these employees were often poorly qualified and even if they had been able to stimulate and assist the Indians in farm work, their number was inadequate. In 1900 there were only 320 farmers to 185,790 Indians, exclusive of the Five Civilized Tribes. ...[106]

Social and Economic Effects of Allotment

The BIA contribution to the Land Planning Report on the social and economic effects of allotment is tragic.

> *The physical liquidation of the Indian landed estate is only one side of the devastation wrought by the allotment system. The effects upon the social and economic condition of the tribe were equally unhappy.* Here are some of the outstanding results of the GAA:

> 1. Allotment broke up the community organization of the tribes as it was frankly intended to do. Tribalism was held in abhorrence by the advocates of allotment. The partition of land in severalty, it was hoped, would dissolve the tribal association and substitute therefor individual status. But

the allotment system thus weakened or destroyed the cohesion of the one unit to which the Indians were culturally attuned - the tribe. In weakening this native means of organization, the allotment theorists assailed the only sound foundation upon which a transformed Indian society could have been built.

2. Allotment shattered family interests and worked as a divisive factor in the lives of all allotted Indians. It did this because allotments were made to the individual and not to the family.

3. *The allotment system, in the manner of its application, attempted to force Indians to become commercial farmers, especially upon the irrigated units.* Many Indians who had been accustomed to sustenance farming were thus forced to attempt commercial farming for which they had little training, knowledge or technology. Thus, whole Indian populations that were known for farming ended up with none of them farming at all.

4. The inheritance of allotments reduced Indian lands to uneconomic units by progressive subdivision. *It transformed Indians into petty landholders and the Office of Indian Affairs into a huge banking and realtor enterprise.*

5. Due to the trust character of Indian allotments, the owners could not pledge their lands for credit, without which it was impossible for them properly to develop their land.

6. Allotment, because of the subdivision produced in heirship status and because of the lack of adequate credit, forced the system of leasing to whites upon the Indians, making of them idlers dependent upon pittances of rental.

7. Allotment led to the creation of a system of probate in the Indian Office which was excessively tardy and unaccountable to the courts.

8. Allotment led directly to making a hundred thousand Indians landless through alienation of land following issuance of fee patents and *failure to provide enough land for future generations*. (Emphasis added)[107]

Allotment's Effects on Grazing and Forest Land

The BIA's contribution to the Land Planning Report on allotment's effect on grazing and forest land is devastating.

> The effects of checkerboarding on potential Indian use of land are especially acute in the case of grazing and forest lands, which constitute 92 percent of all Indian land. *An average Indian allotment of 160 acres of grazing land is much too small to maintain even a subsistence herd of cattle or sheep.* Moreover, for the best utilization and management of grazing lands, it is

essential to have large contiguous areas used in common. On such areas, a minimum of fencing and water development is required, and systematic programs of rotation grazing, range revegetation, erosion control, seasonal grazing, and proper distribution of livestock on the range can be carried out. When a potential Indian grazing range is fragmented into small allotments and minute heirship parcels and further checkerboarded and shared by numerous alienations, the tangle becomes almost hopeless so far as promoting use by Indians is concerned. (Emphasis added)[108]

In the case of Indian forests the problem is even more acute. *Permanent sustained-yield forestry can be practiced in general only on large contiguous areas in one ownership, thus permitting logging and reforestation to progress systematically over natural logging units related to topography and logical transport lines; and ultimately to return, after 50 or 100 years, to renew the cycle at the first point of beginning on the new crop of timber.* Much of the Indian timberland is fragmented by allotment and alienation. Alienated lands, if sufficiently numerous, are an absolute block to sustained yield management; allotted lands are a partial and expensive block. (Emphasis added)[109]

Government's Advocacy for Allotment which Started Early Turned Out to Be "Disastrous"

As early as 1838, the federal government advocated for allotment:

Unless some system is marked out by which there shall be a separate allotment of land to each individual whom the scheme shall entitle to it, you will look in vain for any general casting off of savagism. Common property and civilization cannot co-exist.[110]

The allotment policy was vigorously endorsed within the Indian Service. "The common field is the seat of barbarianism," proclaimed an Indian agent; "the separate farm is the door to civilization." Commissioner of Indian Affairs Oberly explained in 1888, "the Indian must be imbued with the exalting egotism of American civilization so that he will say "I" instead of "We" and "This is mine" instead of "This is ours.""[111]

Commissioner Morgan said in 1892:

If the policy of allotting lands is conceded to be wise, then it should be applied at an early day to all alike wherever the circumstances will warrant. If we have settled upon the breaking up of the tribal relations, the extinguishment of the Indian titles to surplus lands, and the restoration of the unneeded surplus to the public domain, let it be done thoroughly. If reservations have proven to be inadequate for the purposes for which they were designed, have shown themselves a hindrance to the progress of the Indian as well as an obstruction in the pathway of civilization, let the reservations, as speedily as wisdom dictates, be utterly destroyed and entirely swept away.[112]

But Commissioner Francis Leupp reported the severe problems associated with allotment in 1902:

His white brother must bear his proportion of the burden of the Indians' failings. His insatiable greed for "more land," "more free homes," for greater riches, often blind his eyes to the right in dealing with these new-born citizens, who are encompassed by the wily trader, greedy land shark, and heartless money lender. Many white communities around Indian allotted reservations, or "sandwiched" among them, through purchases of inherited lands, fail to cooperate with the Government in holding up the hands of the educated Indians, who have become, in the eyes of the law, their equals. They appear to be unwilling to protect him so long as the Indian has lands to sell or annuities with which to buy. ... The remedy has passed out of Government control; allotment, citizenship, and opening came too soon. It can be seen now. The eastern sentimentalist and the western land grabber unitedly sprung the trap that has been the undoing of the Indians who had lands of value. Greed on the one hand and childishness that looks only to the wants of today on the other hand is completing the work. Retribution-that is not the adequate word-will come at the end of the twenty-five-year probation; when the community will have to bear the burdens of the paupers it has made. Unfortunately, I fear that most of those who have been successful plunderers will escape the responsibility by removing elsewhere. ... This is a gloomy and unfortunately not overdrawn picture. ... In this and similar cases the adult Indians were made citizens before they were ready.[113]

And in 1915, Commissioner Cato Sells stated the truth about the majority of allotments:

I know of many allotments depending entirely upon which an Indian family would starve to death and where no white family could be induced to attempt to make a living, and yet under these circumstances an unsuccessful

Indian farm is apt to be declared a failure. There are thousands of acres of land on Indian reservations where 100 hundred acres would not feed a rabbit.[114]

In 1921, Commissioner Charles H. Burke reported that many allottees lost every acre they had:

> Applications for patents in fee have too often been adroitly supported by influences which sought to hasten the taxable status of the property or to accomplish a purchase at much less than its fair value, or from some other motive foreign to the Indian's ability to protect his property rights. Notwithstanding the sincere efforts of officials and competency commissions to reach a safe conclusion as to the ability of an Indian to manage prudently his business and landed interests, *experience, shows that more than two-thirds of the Indians who have received patents in fee have been unable or unwilling to cope with the business acumen coupled with the selfishness and greed of the more competent whites, and in many instances have lost every acre they had. It is also true that many of the applications received for patents in fee are from those least competent to manage their affairs....*
>
> *The Government should not be expected to shirk its trust.* It should not be made easy for young men to squander their substance and drift into vagrancy, nor for successful landholders to remain under restrictions not justified by their qualifications for citizenship.[115] (Emphasis added)

Commissioner Leupp had no problem in leaving Indians to the sharp business practices of whites. He stated:

> [A]s soon as an Indian of either mixed or full blood becomes capable of taking care of himself, we should set him upon his feet and sever the ties which bind him either to his tribe, in the communal sense, or to the Government. This principle is imperative as to both land and money. ... *[A]fter we have taken our hands off he may fall a victim to sharp practices; but the man never lived-red, white, or any other color-who did not learn a more valuable lesson from one hard blow than from twenty warnings.*[116] (Emphasis added)

The problem is one hard blow could wipe out a whole Indian family's future economic well-being for generations to come.

The severalty policy reduced Indian- owned lands from 155 million acres in 1881 to 77 million in 1900 and just 48 million acres in 1934.[117]

In *Hodel v. Irving*, 481 U.S. 704, 707 (1987), the U.S. Supreme Court declared the allotment policy "disastrous." Within a few decades, the Indian land base had been reduced by two-thirds and reservations were transformed into ungovernable checkerboards of Indian and non-Indian land.

Manifest Destiny Enshrines Land Speculation

Americans declared that it was their manifest destiny to settle and cultivate America's land from the Atlantic to the Pacific, without regard to Indian rights. Land speculators bought large tracts of land with the expectation that it would quickly increase in value as more people settled in the west and demand increased. It was even better if you could get Indian land cheap and re-sell it for a profit.

The Manifest Destiny pushing white settlers westward helped spawn important Euro-American mining, agricultural, ranching and financial ventures. Western businessmen funded by European and eastern capital became millionaires supplying these industries. The financial bounty of Indian nations from their valuable natural resources was siphoned off. Land speculators fed off the hunger of the white settlers who could never dream of land ownership on the European Continent.

An advertisement was prepared in 1911 by Walter L. Fisher, Secretary of Interior, and Robert G. Valentine, Commissioner of Indian Affairs for the sale of Indian lands for grazing and agricultural dry farming with irrigated and irrigable land.[118]

Railroad Companies 'Purchased' Indian Lands for Pennies

Poor's *Manual of Railroads* for 1873 provided as follows regarding railroad land purchases: In 1862, the Atchison & Pike's Peak Railroad purchased 24,000 acres of Kickapoo lands at $1.25 an acre. In October 1867, the Cherokee Neutral Lands were sold to James F. Joy for $1.00 an acre. In May 1868, the Osage Indians sold 8,000,000 acres of their lands to the Leavenworth, Lawrence & Galveston Company at 20 cents an acre. In August 1868, the Atchison, Topeka & Santa Fe Railroad bought 338,766 acres of Potawatomi lands for $1.00 per acre.

Railroad Companies Promoted Land Sales

Railroad companies actively promoted the sale of their land grants to encourage settlement by preparing and placing advertising, including posters, pamphlets and newspaper advertisements, aimed at selling lands, passenger tickets, and the companies' bonds. The companies arranged for production, or produced themselves, advertisements and texts for use in pamphlets and editorial columns. The Union Pacific advertising for the 1868 construction season reportedly cost $200,000.[119]

Much of the railroad grant land was sold to farmers and speculators who bought it at an average price of $4 an acre. The railroads sold their land at a premium in part because they didn't want "poor" farmers locating along their lines, according to John T. Schlebecker. He explained, "A farmer who had so little capital that he could not buy a farm usually could not succeed with a free farm, for homesteaders led the parade of bankrupt farmers. The railroads had no interest in creating zones of poverty along their rights-of-way or in not disposing of their land. They wanted customers with money." For many farmers who bought railroad land, the advantage of being near the railroad more than compensated for the higher price of the land.[120]

The railroads advertised heavily in Europe and brought over, at low fares, hundreds of thousands of farmers from Germany, Scandinavia, and Britain.

Flyers emphasized the lands' fertility and beauty without acknowledging the forced and fraudulent dealings with Indian tribes. An advertisement created by the Burlington & Missouri River Railroad Co. in 1872 was to increase land sales in Iowa and Nebraska promoting "millions of acres" of land being sold on 10 years credit with six percent interest.

The Atchison, Topeka and Santa Fe Railroad distributed posters[121] to encourage land settlement in the Pottawattomie Reserve. Included on the posters was a full page map of the Pottawattomie Reserve on one side and four pictures of the land on the other. The posters/brochures were encouraging farming and settlement in this area because of ready access via the railroad to all markets east of Topeka. Prices and ways to purchase the land were also detailed.

1888: Stereotypes Justifying Mistreatment and Extermination of Indians

Commissioner John N. Oberly, in his Annual Report to the Secretary of Interior in 1888, inscribed the stereotypical view of Indians that dominated federal and state policymaking in the nineteenth century:

The Indian has indeed begun to change with the changing times. He is commencing to appreciate the fact that he must become civilized-must, as he expresses it, "learn the white man's way" - or perish from the face of the earth. He can not sweep back with a broom the flowing tide. The forests into which he ran whooping from the door of "William and Mary" [Indian School in Virginia] have been felled. The game on which he lived has disappeared. The war-path has been obliterated. He is hemmed in on all sides by white population. The railroad refuses to be excluded from his reservation-that hot-bed of barbarism, in which many noxious social and political weeds grow rankly. The Christian missionary is persistently entreating him to abandon paganism. Gradually the paternal hand of the Government is being withdrawn from his support. His environments no longer compel him, or afford to him opportunities, to display the nobler traits of his character. On the war-path and in the chase he was heroic: all activity; patient of hunger; patient of fatigue; coolheaded-a creature of exalted fortitude. But, says a writer, sketching his character, "when the chase was over, when the war was done, and the peace-pipes smoked out, he abandoned himself to debauchery and idleness. To sleep all day in a wig-wam of painted skins, filthy and blackened with smoke, adorned with scalps, and hung with tomahawks and arrows, to dance in the shine of the new moon to music made from the skin of snakes, to tell stories of witches and evil spirits, to gamble, to sing, to jest, to boast of his achievements in war, and to sit with a solemn gravity at the councils of his chiefs constituted his most serious employment. His squaw was his slave. With no more affection than a coyote feels for its mate, he brought her to his wigwam that she might gratify the basest of his passions and minister to his wants. It was Starlight or Cooing Dove that brought the wood for his fire and the water for his drink, that plowed the field and sowed the maize."[122]

These stereotypes became embedded in the consciousness of whites and are still expressed today.

Wisconsin's Indian Holocaust

James Washinawatok, a Menominee attorney, wrote an article about the GAA equaling genocide as defined by the United Nations. What happened in Wisconsin is a tragic repeat of the cycle of cession of Indian lands, removal, establishment of reservations, allotment and opening up "surplus lands" for white settlement. Ceded and surplus lands would be sold, allegedly for the benefit of the affected tribes.

Eliminating one's land base, hence one's control and use of it, destroys all that land encompassed to the people who considered that land home. By physical destruction, a person's life is ended, but by destroying a person's culture, religion, and way of life, they cease to exist as they once did, and not by choice. Tribes physically exist today, but the damage of the GAA is currently experienced almost one-hundred fourteen years later, therefore, a broader definition of genocide is necessary to prevent the further destruction of the GAA.[123]

1889: "Indians Must Conform to 'White Man's Ways,' Peaceably if They Will, Forcibly if They Must"

In 1889, Commissioner T.J. Morgan continued advocacy for the policy of assimilation and allotment:

First. The anomalous position heretofore occupied by the Indians in this country can not much longer be maintained. The reservation system belongs to a "vanishing state of things" and must soon cease to exist. Second. The logic of events demands the absorption of the Indians into our national life, not as Indians, but as American citizens. Third. As soon as a wise conservatism will warrant it, the relations of the Indians to the Government must, rest solely upon the full recognition of their individuality. Each Indian must be treated as a man, be allowed a man's rights …

Fourth. The Indians must conform to "the white man's ways," peaceably if they will, forcibly if they must. They must adjust themselves to their environment, and conform their mode of living substantially to our civilization. This civilization may not be the best possible, but it is the best the Indians can get. They can not escape it, and must either conform to it or be crushed by it.

Sixth. The tribal relations should be broken up, socialism destroyed and the family and the autonomy of the individual substituted. The allotment of lands in severalty, the establishment of local courts and police, the development of a personal sense of independence, and the universal adoption of the English language are means to this end.[124]

Of the land actually acquired 17,400,000 acres, or about one seventh of all the Indian lands in the United States, might seem like a somewhat rapid reduction of the landed estate of the Indians, but when it is considered that for the most part the land relinquished was not being used for any purpose whatever, that scarcely any of it was in cultivation, that the Indians did not need it and would not be likely to need it at any future time, and that they were, as is believed, reasonably well paid for it, the matter assumes quite a different aspect. The sooner the tribal relations are broken up and the reservation system done away with the better it will be for all concerned.[125]

Indian Boarding School Policy

Congress passed legislation in 1889 which allowed the Commissioner of Indian Affairs to enforce the school attendance of Indian children by withholding rations and annuities from Indian families whose children were not attending school.[126]

Commissioner Morgan published a detailed set of rules for Indian schools which stipulated a uniform course of study and the textbooks which were to be used in the schools. Instruction was to include "love of country, obedience to law, respect for civil rulers, fidelity to official trust, obligations of oaths, the ballot, and other duties involved in good citizenship."[127]

On the campus of all the more important schools there should be erected a flagstaff, from which should float constantly, in suitable weather, the American flag. In all schools of whatever size and character, supported wholly or in part by the Government, the "Stars and Stripes" should be a familiar object, and students should be taught to reverence the flag as a symbol of their nation's power and protection.

Patriotic songs should be taught to the pupils, and they should sing them frequently until they acquire complete familiarity with them. Patriotic selections should be committed and recited publicly, and should constitute a portion of the reading exercises.[128]

The 8th of February was to be celebrated as Franchise Day. It was on this day that the Dawes Act was signed into law, and the Commissioner felt that this "is worthy of being observed in all Indian schools as the possible turning point in Indian history, the point at which the Indians may strike out from tribal and reservation life and enter American citizenship and nationality."[129]

In his 1901 Annual Report, Commissioner of Indian Affairs W.A. Jones reported his view of Indian education to the Secretary of Interior:

There are in operation at the present time 113 boarding schools, with an average attendance of something over 16,000 pupils, ranging from 5 to 21 years old. These pupils are gathered from the cabin, the wickiup, and the tepee. Partly by cajolery and partly by threats; partly by bribery and partly by fraud; partly by persuasion and partly by force, they are induced to leave their homes and their kindred to enter these schools and take upon themselves the outward semblance of civilized life. They are chosen not on account of any particular merit of their own, not by reason of mental fitness, but solely because they have Indian blood in their veins. Without regard to their worldly condition; without any previous training; without any preparation whatever, they are transported to the schools-sometimes thousands of miles away-without the slightest expense or trouble to themselves or their people.

The Indian youth finds himself at once, as if by magic, translated from a state of poverty to one of affluence. He is well fed and clothed and lodged. Books and all the accessories of learning are given him and teachers provided to instruct him. He is educated in the industrial arts on the one hand, and not only in the rudiments but in the liberal arts on the other. Beyond "the three r's" he is instructed in geography, grammar, and history; he is taught drawing, algebra and geometry, music, and astronomy, and receives lessons in physiology, botany, and entomology. Matrons wait on him while he is well and physicians and nurses attend him when he is sick. A steam laundry does his washing and the latest modern appliances do his cooking. A library affords him relaxation for his leisure hours, athletic sports and the gymnasium furnish him exercise and recreation, while music entertains him in the evening. He has hot and cold baths, and steam heat and electric light, and all the modern conveniences. All of the necessities of life are given him and many of the luxuries. All of this without money and without price, or the contribution of a single effort of his own or of his people. His wants are all supplied almost for the wish. The child of the wigwam becomes a modern Aladdin, who has only to rub the Government lamp to gratify his desires.

Here he remains until his education is finished, when he is returned to his home-which by contrast must seem squalid indeed-to the parents whom his education must make it difficult to honor, and left to make his way against the ignorance and bigotry of his tribe. Is it any wonder he fails? Is it surprising if he lapses into barbarism? Not having earned his education, it is not appreciated; having made no sacrifice to obtain it, it is not valued. It is looked upon as a right and not as a privilege; it is accepted as a favor to the Government and not to the recipient, and the almost inevitable tendency is to encourage dependence.[130]

In 1928, the Meriam Report—The Problem of Indian Administration—was completed. The Report is particularly critical of the boarding schools: "The survey staff finds itself obligated to say frankly and unequivocally that the provisions for the care of the Indian children in boarding schools are grossly inadequate."[131]

In 2022, Secretary of Interior Deb Haaland described the abuse experienced by Indian children in the boarding schools:

> The purpose of federal Indian boarding schools was to culturally assimilate American Indian, Alaska Native and Native Hawaiian children by forcibly removing them from their families, communities, languages, religions and cultural beliefs. While children attended federal boarding schools, many endured physical and emotional abuse and, in some cases, died.[132]

1903: Unilateral Federal Action to Dispose of Indian Lands

Kiowa leader Lone Wolf sued Secretary of the Interior Ethan Allen Hitchcock to halt the allotment of the Kiowa, Comanche, and Apache Reservation and opening of the surplus lands to non-Indian settlement arguing it violated and abrogated the terms of the Medicine Lodge Treaty of 1867. The U.S. Supreme Court held that Congress could constitutionally break treaties with the tribe because it had absolute, or plenary, power over Indian policy. After *Lone Wolf v. Hitchcock*, 187 U.S. 553 (1903), Congress immediately began to change the way that it dealt with Indian property. Commissioner of Indian Affairs William Jones in testimony before the House Indian Affairs Committee stated: "The decision in the *Lone Wolf* case will enable you to dispose of [Indian] land without the consent of the Indians. If you wait for their consent in these matters, it will be fifty years before you can do away with the reservations." … "Supposing you were the guardian or ward of a child 8 or 10 years of age," he told, "would you ask the consent of a child as to the investment of its funds? No; you would not."[133] Congress followed Jones' suggestion and, without even initiating negotiations, proceeded to adopt allotment statutes for many Indian reservations.

Indian Reorganization Act ("IRA") Trust System Inaugurated

The Native American Heritage website of the National Archives provides a short, concise summary of the Indian Reorganization Act ("IRA"):

> The IRA led to major changes related to tribal land ownership and self-government. The IRA ended allotment of tribal lands, which had broken apart reservations and led to serious economic and cultural impacts on

tribal communities, and established a process by which lands could be restored to tribal ownership.

The act also recognized tribal governments and offered incentives for tribes to adopt U.S. government-style constitutions and governing councils. In addition to these major policy shifts, the IRA set aside funds for Indian education and established Indian hiring preference in the Bureau of Indian Affairs (BIA).

For its supporters, the IRA was a major victory in preserving and strengthening tribal sovereignty, which had been undermined by decades of forced assimilation into American society.

For its critics, however, the IRA ignored differences in American Indian and Alaska Native cultures and their traditional methods of organization and leadership.

The IRA extended the trust period on allotments indefinitely. It charged the Secretary of Interior with the authority to take new lands into trust for tribes, helping to stem the tide of land loss. Even so, it did not eliminate that problem. The "takings" of Indian lands continued through the 1930s and 40s as government entities seized lands for infrastructure uses such as dams and other water projects, railroads and highways.

Though the IRA abolished the practice of allotting land, nearly 50 years of allotment had created an ownership maze on many reservations that included individual trust land, tribal trust land, fee land, and alienated land owned by various non-Indian entities. Over the years, the trust land ownership interests had become increasingly fractionated and difficult to manage. IRA Tribes are those who voted to accept the Indian Reorganization Act (IRA) of 1934.

7: TERMINATION; SELF-DETERMINATION

Termination

Termination was a U.S. government policy aimed at ending federal supervision over American Indian tribes.

Officially announced on August 1, 1953, in House Concurrent Resolution 108 (67 Stat. 132), termination was expressly intended to "make Indians within the territorial limits of the United States subject to the same laws and entitled to the same privileges and responsibilities as are applicable to other citizens of the United States, to end their status as wards of the United States, and to grant them all of the rights and prerogatives pertaining to American citizenship." This was despite the fact that American Indians had been U.S. citizens since Congress passed the Indian Citizenship Act in 1924. (43 Stat. 253).

Termination was a departure from federal Indian policy in the 1930s and early 1940s, during which time the U.S. government ceased allotting tribal reservations and emphasized tribal self-government instead. Termination ended federal recognition of affected tribes and the federal aid and services that came with that recognition. It also ended federal trust status for affected reservations and the protections granted by such status.

There were 109 tribes and bands whose federal recognition was terminated.

Although the Nixon administration repudiated termination in 1970 and shifted federal Indian policy toward self-determination, the effect of termination was nevertheless devastating for many tribes.[134]

1968: New Era of Indian Self-Determination

1968: President Lyndon B. Johnson, Indian Self-Determination

Lyndon B. Johnson, "Special Message to Congress on the Problems of the American Indian: The Forgotten American," March 6, 1968

> I propose a new goal for our Indian programs: *A goal that ends the old debate about 'termination' of Indian programs and stresses self-determination*... The greatest hope for Indian progress lies in the emergence of Indian leadership and initiative in solving Indian problems. *Indians must have a voice in making the plans and decisions in programs which are important to their daily life*. ... (Emphasis added)

1970: President Richard M. Nixon, Indian Self-Determination

In a Special Message to Congress on Indian Affairs, President Richard Nixon denounced the Eisenhower-era policy of terminating Indian nations and announced a policy under which "the Indian future is determined by Indian acts and Indian decisions."

Successive Presidential Administrations Confirmed Tribal Sovereignty and Right to Self-Determination

Successive Presidential administrations have affirmed this policy of protecting the integrity of tribal governments through the maintenance of federal-tribal government-to-government relationships.

Ronald Reagan, Indian Policy Statement, January 24, 1983

William Clinton, "Government-to-Government Relations with Native American Tribal Governments: Memorandum for the Heads of Executive Departments and Agencies," April 29, 1994

George W. Bush, Memorandum for the Heads of Executive Departments and Agencies, "Government-to-Government Relationship With Tribal Governments," September 2004

Barack Obama, Tribal Nations Conference, U.S. Department of Interior, Washington, DC, November 5, 2009

Joseph Biden, Executive Order 14112 on Reforming Federal Funding and
Support for Tribal Nations to Better Embrace Our Trust Responsibilities
and Promote the Next Era of Tribal Self-Determination, December 6,
2023.

Tribal Consultation Ordered: President Biden's November 22, 2022, Memorandum

President Biden's 2022 Memorandum ordering Tribal Consultation expresses the unique, legally affirmed Nation-to-Nation relationship with American Indian and Alaska Native Tribal Nations and affirms the principles of Tribal Sovereignty, Self-Determination and Self-Governance.

8: Indian Allotment Probate Legislation and Implementation

Department of Interior's ("DOI") Tribal and Indian Individual Probate Trust Responsibilities

The U.S. holds legal title to over 10 million acres of land for the benefit of individual Indians. Most, but not all, of these lands are located within Indian reservation boundaries. They are often leased out for grazing, oil and gas development, or other income-generating activities. The DOI collects some $300 million in revenue a year on the lands, and distributes it to hundreds of thousands of individual Indian beneficiaries.

The DOI's trust responsibilities consist of the highest moral obligations that the U.S. must meet to ensure the protection of tribal and individual Indian lands, assets, resources, and treaty and similarly recognized rights. The BIA is responsible for carrying out the bulk of the federal government's trust responsibilities to individual Indians and tribes. The BIA manages Indian lands and resources, and plays a central role in the probate of Indian estates, along with the OHA, Probate Hearings Division ("PHD"), DOI.

As stated by the Department of Justice: "The Department of the Interior (Interior) has a continuing responsibility to provide adequate staffing, supervision and training for trust fund management and accounting." (25 U.S.C. Sec. 162 a(d) (7)).[135]

1983: Indian Land Consolidation Act ("ILCA")

In 1983, Congress passed the Indian Land Consolidation Act ("ILCA") in an attempt to slow the rapidly growing fractionation of trust lands. ILCA authorized tribes to draft their own land consolidation plans and probate codes which could limit inheritance by non-Indians and non-tribal members. The provision in ILCA that required small fractional interests to revert to the tribes was declared unconstitutional. Amendments to ILCA passed in 2000 were never fully implemented. ILCA ended up being so complex that the DOI ultimately conceded that the law was too complicated to administer.[136]

2003: Billion Dollar Truth about Fractionation

In 2003, Mr. Ross Swimmer, Special Trustee, warned that *it may become impossible* to manage the fractionated Indian estates that existed then, even with a budget of billions of dollars. While AIPRA was intended to address this problem, the fractionation solution alone is not the issue, it as Mr. Swimmer stated, "reengineer[ing] the core trust business processes." This is still a problem today.

> The fractionated nature of the individual Indian land has been discussed at great length in many articles and reports during the last century and continuing today. Past fractionation remains a serious problem that requires innovative thinking. The cost of purchasing fractionated interests is estimated to be in the billions of dollars, yet the ongoing cost of managing fractionated interests will, in the long-term, cost much more or may even become impossible. I believe the solution to this problem will come from continued dialogue among Interior, Tribes, individual allottees and Congress. ... Regardless of Interior's best effort to reengineer the core trust business processes, until such issues as fractionation are resolved, trust reform will remain difficult to achieve. Maintaining thousands of accounts with balances of less than one dollar could not have been envisioned when Congress enacted the General Allotment Act of 1887. *Date: October 29, 2003, Ross O. Swimmer, Special Trustee for American Indians.*

1929: Urgent Probate Issues Recognized

Commissioner Charles J. Rhoads documented the urgency of this matter in a letter to Senator Lynn Frazier in 1929.

> The indefinite partitioning of allotments is not practicable; the Indian heir who may desire to remain on his allotment and cultivate it rarely would be able to buy out those heirs who might desire a liquidation of the heirship estate.

> The consequences are mathematically certain: the allotted Indians of the second generation largely become landless. By the time the third generation

has arrived, substantially all of the allotted Indian land will have passed into white ownership. What this means is appreciated when it is noted that the Indian allotted land constitutes more than one-half of the whole area of Indian country and much more than half of the surface value of Indian country, and when it is further noted that more than two-thirds of the Indians are now allotted....

I make the very tentative suggestion that part, at least, of the loss of Indian heirship land to the Indians might be averted if there were some means provided whereby the allotted land could revert to the tribal estate. ... It has been suggested that Indian tribes might be permitted and assisted to form themselves into corporate bodies and that allotments might be turned back into the tribal estate in exchange for shares of stock. Such a method, it would seem, might be practicable for those reservations possessed of large tribal assets, such as timber, oil, minerals, or water power. ... Letter from Commissioner C. J. Rhoads to Senator Lynn Frazier, December 11, 1929, in Wheeler-Howard Act—exempt Certain Indians: Hearings Before the Committee on Indian Affairs, House of Representatives, Seventy-sixth Congress, Third Session, on S. 2103, 1940, p. 25.

Indivisible Tribal Estate

Sec. of Interior Wilbur further discussed this matter in a letter to Senator Lynn Frazier in 1929:

We are confronted with the problem of what to do with the indivisible tribal estates of the Indians. *There are conditions with which it seems impossible to deal satisfactorily under existing law. ... Indian wealth totaling hundreds of millions of dollars—possibly a billion dollars—is essentially indivisible.* It includes such items as mineral and oil resources, power sites, timber wealth, the large bodies of grazing land, and even the farm lands...

At present and under existing law the Government, through the Interior Department, is charged with the direct and highly paternalistic administration of these properties, and *unless existing law be changed it may well be that the Government 100 years from now will find itself still charged with this responsibility and still maintaining the paternalistic administration.*

As I have stated, under existing law the Government may find itself administering these vast and varied properties to the end of time. And through all this time the Indians, so far as existing law is concerned, must remain in a state of dependency, being neither forced nor permitted to take on the business responsibilities of American life or to make use of the instrumentalities of modern business. (Emphasis added) Letter from Sec. of Interior Wilbur to Senator Lynn Frazier, in *Congressional Record*, 1931, Part 4, 74:3980-3981.

Commissioner Nash followed up on this in his address at the 18th Annual Convention of the National Congress of American Indians, September 21, 1961. https://www.bia.gov/as-ia/opa/online-press-release/address-nash-annual-convention-ncai (accessed online March 11, 2024).

> One of the most pressing of all Indian land problems is that which follows from the multiple ownership of land which has passed undivided to heirs of an allottee. There are now more than 10 percent of the total Indian estate— and of this land nearly a half a million acres have been found by the Senate Committee on Interior and Indian Affairs to be unproductive because of multiple ownership. Generally speaking, there are so many owners that the consent of all of them cannot be obtained to a lease.

> There are some instances of checks being drawn for just a few cents. Such income means very little to the Indian owner. The cost of managing it is out of reason and brings severe criticism from Congress and from Indian groups and friends of the Indians. The solution of this problem will not wait upon our convenience. A solution is needed now.

AIPRA Process for Trust Property

> The AIPRA changed the procedures related to the inheritance of trust lands. Among its purposes is preserving the trust status of Indian lands by restricting non-Indian inheritance, reducing fractionation by earmarking federal funds for consolidation, and authorizing Indian co-owner and tribal purchase and sale of ownership interests.[137]

In hearing witnesses on the bill, Statement of The Honorable Nick J. Rahall, II, Ranking Democrat, Committee on Resources, stated as follows:

> To be frank, slogging through the bill pending before us today is a tedious

chore. With terms like "pendency of probate," "after-born heirs," and "revocation of owner-managed status," this is a bill only a probate lawyer and the greeneyeshade folks can love. What is not a chore, however, is looking into the faces of Indian Country whose very family and tribal traditions depend on how we respond to the land crisis this bills seeks to address. ... We must ensure Indian lands stay in Indian hands and in trust status.[138]

AIPRA does not apply to the Five Civilized Tribes or the Osage Nation's trust or restricted lands. Separate rules may apply to Alaska and California tribes.

There is an amended definition of Indian that helps determine who can inherit an interest in land in trust, particularly where there is no will. Under AIPRA, an "Indian" is a person who:

Is a member of an Indian tribe, or
Is eligible to become a member of an Indian tribe; or
Was an owner of an interest in trust or restricted land on October 27, 2004; or
Meets the definition of "Indian" under the Indian Reorganization Act, or
In California, any person as in 1, 2, 3, and 4, or who owns trust or restricted land in California.

Eligible heirs are also defined by AIPRA:

The decedent's children, grandchildren, great grandchildren, full siblings, half siblings by blood and parents who are (a) Indian; or (b) lineal descendents within 2 degrees of consanguinity of an Indian; or (c) owners of a trust or restricted interest in a parcel of land for purposes of inheriting by descent, renunciation, or consolidation agreement under section 2206, another trust or restricted interest in such parcel from the descendent. 25 U.S.C. § 2201(9).

Also, under AIPRA, land is defined as any real property including improvements permanently affixed to it, such as a barn or house.

DOI's Indian Probate Process

Trust lands and Individual Indian Money ("IIM") Accounts are probated by the OHA. Tribal and State courts cannot probate trust property.

The Congressional Research Service reported the following on January 29, 2024, on The Department of the Interior's Tribal Probate Process: In Brief:

DOI's regulations define probate as "the legal process by which applicable tribal, federal, or state law that affects the distribution of a decedent's estate is applied" to:

Determine the heirs;
Determine the validity of wills and determine devisees;
Determine whether claims against the estate will be paid from trust personalty; and order the transfer of any trust or restricted land or trust personalty to the heirs, devisees, or other persons or entities entitled by law to receive them. 25 C.F.R. §15.2.[139]

There are numerous sources online explaining this process and AIPRA's impact. For example, the DOI has sources such as *Your Land Your Decision. What is a Probate? A Guide to help American Indians & Alaska Natives* as a help to understand the Department of the Interior's (DOI) Probate Process. https://www.bia.gov/bia/ots/dop/your-land (accessed online February 11, 2024) (herein "Your Land Your Decision"). See also The National Congress of American Indians A Quick Guide to the American Indian Probate Reform Act online at https://iltf.org/wp-content/uploads/2016/11/A-Quick-Guide-to-AIPRA-NCAI.pdf (accessed online February 11, 2024).

2024: BIA Backlog of More Than 32,000 Indian Probate Cases

The BIA estimated that heading into FY2024, it had a probate case **backlog of more than 32,000 cases.** (Emphasis added)[140] This backlog is interfering with the DOI's trust responsibilities. As stated by the Indian Land Tenure Foundation: It is not uncommon for an heir to a deceased person's estate to pass on before the original probate is resolved.

COVID Backlog

The onset and long duration of the COVID-19 pandemic exacerbated this backlog as did the government shutdown, and a delay in hiring judges. Several rural offices had to be temporarily closed due to the COVID-19 intensity. In addition, the COVID-19 pandemic halted travel in order to protect the health and well-being of elders and others in the Indian community.[141]

Judicial Cases Requiring Reopening Closed Indian Probate Cases

Probates are still being reopened as a result of the 1996 U.S. Supreme Court decision in the *Babbitt v. Youpee, Sr.* case requiring the return of fractionated interests taken from heirs without payment. This complicates the process and causes further probate backlog as cases are reopened to determine rightful heirs for redistribution of fractional interests.

The *Cobell v. Norton* Indian trust litigation, 428 F.3d 1070 (D.D.C. 2005), which was started in 1996 and settled in 2011 required reopening closed cases to determine rightful heirs for redistribution of fractional interests and monies.

Building and Implementing a Trust Services Delivery System

Interior's Annual Status Reports, required by judicial order, in *Cobell v. Norton,* Case No. 1:96CV01285, recognized the problems before and after AIPRA. The major obstacles have not shifted.

Major obstacles affecting the ability of Interior to build and implement a trust services delivery model include:

The sheer complexity of reengineering the existing trust business processes to achieve integrated and consistent business processes;
The cost and complexity of managing highly fractionated land interests and the resulting extremely numerous and small accounts.[142]

Interior's Fifteenth Status Report in 2003 had a section by the BIA specifically listing what it considered its obstacles were:

Lack of consistent staffing in program management;
Lack of adequate staffing for probate processing in the field;
Lack of a comprehensive case management and tracking system;
Fractionation of ownership of Indian lands;
Numerous title initiatives (*Youpee* re-vestitures, *Cobell* initiatives).[143]

2024: BIA Indian Probate Action Plan

The BIA committed in FY 2024 to the following:

Develop a journey map outlining the probate process: With input from beneficiaries and employees, the journey map will help BIA to identify and prioritize pain points, collect beneficiary feedback, and improve training for probate staff.

Identify data sharing collaborations with government and Tribal agencies: **BIA *will review potential collaborations with states*,** Tribal governments, and Federal entities (e.g., Social Security Administration, Indian Health Service) to share data and documents to streamline the probate process and minimize burden of beneficiaries.

Improve the account closing process for distributing cash trust assets: With the Bureau of Trust Funds Administration, BIA will implement a new module to distribute cash assets more quickly. (Emphasis added)[144]

AIPRA Federal Indian Probate Code Replaces State Law

One of the key provisions of AIPRA is the establishment of a uniform federal probate code that replaces state law in probating Indian trust land and assets. This code applies where no valid will or applicable tribal probate code exists.

AIPRA: Two Categories of Individual Indian Trust Land and Intestacy Rules Applicable to Each Category

To reduce the further fractionation of trust land interests when the decedent dies without a will, AIPRA divides land interests into two categories: those interests 5 percent or greater and those interests less than 5 percent of the total allotted parcel. 25 U.S.C. § 2206(a).

AIPRA then applies different intestacy rules to each category. Again, this is when a decedent owning trust land dies without a will.

Excellent Charts on Understanding AIPRA for Landowners by the Indian Land Tenure Foundation's Institute for Indian Estate Planning & Probate at Seattle University School of Law are available online at: https://iltf.org/wp-content/uploads/2016/11/Understanding-AIRPA-For-Landowners-Institute.pdf (accessed online March 14, 2024).

Individual Indian Trust Land Interests Greater Than 5% Without a Will

Your trust land will continue to be inherited by your immediate family— first to your children or grandchildren or possibly great grandchildren, and if you have none, then to your parents or brothers and sisters. All of these people will be eligible to inherit your trust property as long as each meets the definition of Indian, or are your descendants within two generations of an Indian, or they already are co-owners in the same parcel. Land not passing to one of the people above will then pass to the tribe where the land is located.[145]

Interests are given to the surviving spouse in a life estate, allowing the spouse to receive all income from the land, and continue to live on or use the land, until the spouse dies. When a non-Indian spouse dies, all interests greater than 5% go equally to the surviving eligible children in undivided interests. If there are no children, then interests go to grandchildren or others.

If a child has died before the decedent, that child's eligible children will share that interest equally.

If none, the interests will pass to the decedent's surviving eligible grandchildren or greatgrandchildren in equal shares. 25 U.S.C. § 2206(a)(2)(B)(ii).

If none, the interests will pass to the decedent's surviving eligible parents in equal shares. 25 U.S.C. § 2206(a)(2)(B)(iii).

If no parents, then the interest shall pass to the decedent's surviving eligible siblings in equal shares. 25 U.S.C. § 2206(a)(2)(B)(iv).

If none, the interests will go to the Indian tribe with jurisdiction over the lands. 25 U.S.C. § 2206(a)(2)(B)(v).[146]

An excellent chart for probating Estates of Individual Indian Trust Land Interests Greater Than 5% Without a Will is available online at: AIPRA for Landowners, Indian Land Tenure Foundation's Institute for Indian Estate Planning & Probate at Seattle University School of Law. https://iltf.org/wp- or-Landowners-Institute. pdf (accessed online March 14, 2024).

Individual Indian Trust Land Interests Less Than 5% Without a Will

The probate court will give the spouse a life estate in only the trust property that was being lived on at the landowner's time of death. All other interests less than 5% will go to a "single heir," the oldest surviving child or grandchild. If there are no surviving children or grandchildren, interests go to the tribe with jurisdiction or to any co-owners in that allotment if there is no tribe, and if none, then to the Secretary of the Interior for sale. 25 U.S.C. § 2201(3).

A surviving spouse will receive nothing, unless the spouse is living on that interest at the time of the decedent's death, and even then the spouse will only receive a life estate. 25 U.S.C. § 2206(a)(2)(D)(ii).

It makes no difference if the surviving spouse is Indian, non-Indian, or otherwise an heir eligible—a surviving spouse will never receive more than a life estate. 25 U.S.C. § 2206(a)(2)(A); 25 U.S.C. § 2206(a)(2)(D).

The life estate provided by AIPRA is without regard to waste, allowing the spouse to live on and use that interest of land for his or her lifetime, including all income and revenue generated from it. 25 U.S.C. § 2201(10).

Once the spouse dies, the interest will transfer to the single heir as designated above. 25 U.S.C. § 2206(a)(2)(D)(ii).

An excellent chart for probating Estates of Individual Indian Trust Land Interests Less Than 5% Without a Will is available online at: AIPRA for Landowners, Indian Land Tenure Foundation's Institute for Indian Estate Planning & Probate at Seattle University School of Law. https://iltf.org/wp-content/uploads/2016/11/Understanding-AIRPA-For-Landowners-Institute.pdf (accessed online March 14, 2024).

Additionally, the DOI may purchase interests in land that are less than 5% of the total for fair market value during the probate proceeding without the consent of the heirs.

Three things will preclude a forced sale at the probate of interests less than 5 percent: (1) the interest is passing by a valid will, thus triggering the consent requirement; [25 U.S.C. § 2206(o)(5)(A)(i)] (2) the interest is passing intestate, but the heir to receive it lives on that parcel at the time of the decedent's death; [25 U.S.C. § 2206(o)(5)(B)(i)] or (3) the heirs voluntarily agree to enter into a consolidation agreement at probate. [25 U.S.C. § 2206(e)].[147]

Individual Indian Money ("IIM") Accounts in Intestacy Proceedings

IIM Accounts contain money collected from leases, minerals, timber sales etc., from land in which Indians own interests. The accounts are administered by the Office of the Special Trustee ("OST") within the DOI.[148]

If you have a spouse and other eligible heirs, your surviving spouse will inherit 1/3 of any money in your IIM account at the time of your death, and all of the money produced from your interest in trust or restricted land during your spouse's lifetime. Your other heirs get the remaining 2/3 of any money in your IIM account at the time of death, and the remaining ownership interest in the trust or restricted land. Your spouse may also continue to live in a family home located on allotted land. If your spouse but no other eligible heirs survive you, the spouse gets your IIM account, and during the spouse's lifetime, the money produced from your land interest. The spouse may also continue to live in a family home located on allotted land. The remaining ownership interest in land goes to the tribe where the land is located.

An excellent chart for probating Individual Indian Money ("IIM") Accounts in Intestacy Proceedings is available online at: Understanding AIPRA for Landowners, Indian Land Tenure Foundation's Institute for Indian Estate Planning & Probate at Seattle University School of Law. https://iltf.org/wp-content/uploads/2016/11/Understanding-AIRPA-For-Landowners-Institute.pdf (accessed online March 14, 2024).

DOI on Need for Legal Advice in Indian Probate Proceedings

The DOI states on the Your Land Your Decision site:

> *Probate laws can and do change and are sometimes complex. Each case is unique and may have special factors; therefore, if you want professional advice for your legal situation you should seek the advice and counsel of an attorney.* (Emphasis added)

The problem is that many Indians cannot afford retaining an attorney. This is fully recognized by all agencies within the executive branch. This can delay probating Indian estates and even of more concern, infringe on the rights of Indian actual or potential heirs.

Indian Probate Attorney Jared Miller's Blog Addresses Difficult Legal Issues

Sometimes prospective clients ask me whether they even need a lawyer at a federal Indian probate hearing. Often someone at the Bureau of Indian Affairs (BIA) has told them that they don't need counsel, and the prospective client calls me to make sure. The question is getting harder to answer.

In the past, parties could represent themselves in the early stages of the probate and hire a lawyer to seek rehearing if they made mistakes. But regulations released in January make it harder for lawyers to fix those errors.

The fact is Native American probate is becoming more complex and some new rules are less forgiving to unrepresented parties. Lawyers provide an invaluable service to prospective clients when they can explain these risks without pushing prospective clients to hire them in cases where lawyers truly aren't required.[149]

Two-Thirds of IBIA Pro Se Cases Dismissed

In discussing "the complex federal legal system used to probate land and money that the U.S. government holds in trust on behalf of Native Americans," Mr. Miller discusses the lack of lawyers and the problems due to this as well as Indians representing themselves:

> The numbers tell the tale. In 2023, two-thirds of pro se cases [were] dismissed.
>
> In 2022, the Interior Board of Indian Appeals (IBIA), the body that hears appeals from Indian probate cases, issued 11 opinions in such cases but reached the merits only twice. In 2021, the IBIA reached the merits twice in 20 probate cases. In other words, the *IBIA docketed 31 Indian probate cases in the last two years and reached the merits only four times.*
>
> *It dismissed most of those cases for procedural errors, like problems with service and missed deadlines, or for failure to prosecute—all problems that competent counsel could have avoided.*[150] (Emphasis added)

Getting Copy of Indian Probate Case File

Interested parties rarely see their federal probate case files. Before AIPRA, it was unclear whether parties had a right to view their files at all. Today, they are able to request the files if they do so in writing, although most probably do not know this. When files are requested, they sometimes arrive long after the initial hearing. A system more devoted to due process would guarantee that a copy of the file is delivered to each interested party along with the notice of initial hearing.

The probate process is highly technical, which limits due process. Nonetheless, "parties to a probate proceeding are presumed to have knowledge of the regulations governing those proceedings." *Estate of John Martin Red Bear*, 41 IBIA 273, 275 (2005). ***Frankly, many of our clients and former clients express fear and apprehension about the prospect of representing themselves in probate matters—let alone gaining mastery of the law and regulations beforehand.*** (Emphasis added)[151]

Per Mr. Miller:

What's the first thing you do after agreeing to represent a party in a federal Indian probate case? You request a copy of the probate file from the Office of Hearings and Appeals (OHA). Even then, the file probably won't arrive in time for the initial hearing; you might go in blind.

Then you'll have to convince the judge to set a supplemental hearing and hope the file arrives before then. Judge's like to probate estates at the initial hearing if possible, so come prepared with a good reason to delay.

Once you get the file, you can prepare your case.[152]

IBIA May Dismiss Case Without Addressing Merits

The IBIA may dismiss a case without addressing the merits.

25 CFR § 2.503 May an appeal be dismissed without a decision on the merits? Yes, the reviewing official may dismiss an appeal without a decision on the merits when: (a) You are late in filing your appeal; (b) You lack standing because you do not meet the requirements of § 2.200 for bringing an appeal; (c) You have withdrawn the appeal; (d) You have failed to pay a required appeal bond; (e) The reviewing official lacks the authority to grant the requested relief; (f) If you are represented and your representative does not meet the standards established in 43 CFR part 1 related to eligibility to practice before the Department, and you have failed to substitute yourself or an eligible representative after being given an opportunity to do so; or (g) The reviewing official determines there are other circumstances that warrant a dismissal and explains those circumstances in the dismissal order.[153]

Bad Time to Appeal to Interior Board of Indian Appeals

Now is a bad time to make mistakes in federal Indian probate cases. That's because the Interior Board of Indian Appeals (IBIA) is taking about five years to deliver substantive opinions in probate cases. Nobody wants to get stuck in that quagmire.[154]

Dismissal Based on Procedural Errors

2024: Estate of Little Owl: Failure to Serve Notice of Appeal ("NOA") on Interested Parties

> In 1976, Administrative Law Judge Daniel S. Boos entered a decision that determined Decedent's heirs and distributed his trust estate. (Internal citations omitted).

> Appellant petitioned to reopen Decedent's estate and add his father Aaron as a child and heir of Decedent. The IPJ denied Appellant's petition for reopening.

> The probate regulations allow a probate case to be reopened to correct an error, but if it has been closed for more than 3 years, the IPJ may reopen the case only if he finds that "the need to correct the error outweighs the interests of the public and heirs or devisees in the finality of the probate proceeding." In deciding whether that standard is met, the IPJ will consider, to the extent applicable, factors set forth in the regulations. These include: (1) "[w]hether the interested party exercised due diligence in pursuing his or her rights" and (2) "[w]hether the interested party's ancestor exercised due diligence in pursuing his or her rights and whether a failure to exercise should be imputed to the interested party."

> *(1) Appellant did not serve the parties listed on the distribution list; (2) under our regulations, service must be made by mail or personal delivery (and only by electronic transmission under certain circumstances that do not apply here); and (3) Appellant did not include a copy of his notice of appeal in those messages. We warned Appellant that this appeal might be dismissed without further notice if he failed to complete service, and he has not done so ...* see also *Estate of Faith Edith Black Horse*, 49 IBIA 196, 196-97 (2009) (dismissing appeal for failure to comply with an order to serve the notice of appeal on interested parties). (Emphasis added)

Untimely Filing of NOA: Due 30 Days from Date Order Was Mailed

Connie L. Filesteel (Appellant) appealed to the Board of Indian Appeals ... in the estate of Edward Filesteel, Sr. (Decedent), deceased Fort Belknap Indian ... (Internal citations omitted).

On receipt of the appeal, because it appeared that Appellant's appeal may have been untimely, the Board ordered Appellant to submit evidence of the date of mailing her notice of appeal to the Board. Pre-Docketing Notice, Order to Submit Original Signed Notice of Appeal, and Order to Submit Evidence of Mailing Notice of Appeal, October 18, 2023.

According to Appellant, this language in the certificate "would include the Board of Indian Appeals' ... copy, since I confused which office was to receive the original Notice of Appeal."

Because Appellant asserts that she simultaneously sent copies of the notice of appeal to the Board and BIA by placing copies in a "night drop box," and the copies that Appellant sent to the Fort Belknap Agency and the LTRO were postmarked 1 day after the October 10, 2023, filing deadline, the Board concludes that Appellant's response does not satisfy her burden of proof to show that she mailed her notice of appeal to the Board on or before October 10, 2023.

An appeal from a probate judge's order must be filed with the Board within 30 days from the date the order was mailed with accurate appeal instructions. ... Untimely appeals must be dismissed. The Board does not have authority to extend the time period for filing an appeal. Estate of Wilfred Charles Kozevnikoff, 62 IBIA 15 (2015). (Emphasis added)

In another example, Mr. Miller states:

Last week, the Interior Board of Indian Appeals (IBIA) dismissed an appeal in a federal Indian probate case because a woman tried to represent herself without an attorney and missed the filing deadline by three days. The consequences of a missed appeal deadline are devastating because, "[t]he [IBIA] does not have authority to grant an extension for filing a notice." Estate of Robert Roy Ahenakew, Jr., 68 IBIA 147, 148 (2022).[155]

Indian Education Problems Exist in Urban and Rural Areas: Makes Maze of Indian Probate Process More Difficult, If Not Impossible, to Navigate

While it may seem out of place, the education difficulties faced by Indians is an important factor to consider. It makes the maze of the Indian probate process more difficult, if not impossible, to navigate.

In 1978 in The Indian Student Amid American Inconsistencies, Vine Deloria, Jr., with incredible clarity, elucidates on Indian education:

> Indian Education has been built upon the premise that the Indian had a great deal to learn from the white man; the white man representing the highest level of achievement reached in the evolutionary process. The white man's religion was the best, his economics superior, his sense of justice the keenest, his knowledge of history the greatest. The Indian's task was to consume bits and pieces of the white man's world in the expectation that some day he would become as smart. The totality of the white man's knowledge was supposed to encompass the wisdom of the ages, painfully accumulated by a series of brilliant men.[156]

Colorado is used as an example to provide probative information.

This accumulation of the "white man's knowledge" has bypassed the state of Colorado. In 2020, in startling statistics for 11th grade students, **Only 29.2% of American Indian or Alaska Native Students Met or Exceeded Expectations on *English* standardized testing and Only 19.0% of American Indian or Alaska Native Students Met or Exceeded Expectations in Math.**[157] (Emphasis added)

Lack of Understanding Evident in IBIA Pro Se Cases Resulting in Inability to State Grounds for Petition

The *Estate of Margaret Jo Brown,* 69 IBIA 222 (12/06/2023), is an example of the lack of understanding regarding the probate procedural grounds. (Internal citations omitted). The IBIA stated as follows:

> Appellant seeks review of a Notice of Filing of Petition for Rehearing by Earlicia Brown and Order Denying Rehearing. *When Appellant sought rehearing, it was her burden to allege an error of fact or law in the Decision and state specifically and concisely the grounds on which the petition was based. The September 18 facsimile states only: "We file a rehearing. Sincerely, Earlicia Brown." The September 20 letter adds only a reference to Decedent's estate, merely stating: "We file a rehearing in Margaret [B]rown estate. Sincerely, Earlicia Brown." ... Further, any claim against Decedent's estate was required to have been filed "before the conclusion of the first hearing." Claims that are not so filed are barred.* (Emphasis added)

Inability to Understand Legal Terminology Such as "Show Cause"

In the *Estate of John M. Grandboise*, 68 IBIA 195 (07/20/2022), the IBIA dismissed the appeal for failure to show cause. It is unlikely the Appellant knew what show cause means. "An order to show cause (O.S.C.), is a court order or the demand of a judge requiring a party to justify or explain why the court should or should not grant a motion or a relief."[158] The case stated:

> Upon receipt of the appeal, the Board ordered Appellant to complete service of her notice of appeal on the IPJ and interested parties … and to notify the Board that she had done so. In addition, the Board ordered Appellant to show cause why the Board should not dismiss the appeal or summarily affirm the Rehearing Order because Appellant failed to respond to an order by the IPJ to show cause why the will should not be approved and because Appellant's notice of appeal did not appear to allege any grounds upon which the Board could find error in the IPJ's decision.

Appeal Mailed to PHD Field Office, Not IBIA; Dismissed as Untimely

On April 19, 2022, the Board of Indian Appeals (Board) received a letter from Billie Jo Potts (Appellant), pro se. … Appellant sent her letter to the PHD's office in Billings, Montana. PHD transmitted the letter to the Board … **We construe the letter as a notice of appeal from the Order Denying Reopening. We docket the appeal but dismiss it as untimely because the IPJ provided accurate appeal instructions, the appeal was not filed with the Board within the 30-day deadline following the IPJ's Order Denying Reopening, and the Board lacks authority to extend the time for filing a notice of appeal.** *Estate of Robert Roy Ahenakew, Jr.*, 68 IBIA 147 (04/26/2022). (Emphasis added)

Appeal Mailed to PHD Field Office, Not IBIA; Lack of Standing; Failure to Prosecute

Appellant sent her appeal to the Probate Hearings Division office in Albuquerque, New Mexico (PHD), and PHD forwarded it to the Board. It was untimely.

In the *Estate of Nathan Bruce Doyeb*, 68 IBIA 192 (07/20/2022), the IBIA dismissed the case for "lack of standing" and "failure to prosecute." These are "terms of art." A term of art means "a word or phrase that has a specific or precise meaning within a given discipline or field and might have a different meaning in common usage..." Standing is defined as follows: You have a right to appeal a decision made by an Indian Affairs official if you can show, *through credible statements*, that you are adversely affected.

> Testimony that is credible (i.e., believable) doesn't mean it must be wholly accepted as the truth. A factfinder may resolve factual issues against a party without expressly finding that party not credible. This is a regular, non-controversial occurrence in everyday litigation. (*Ming Dai v. Barr*, 940 F.3d 1143 (9th Cir. 2019)).

The IBIA has defined "failure to prosecute" as follows:

> Whenever a record discloses the failure of either party to file documents required by these rules, respond to notices or correspondence from the presiding officer, comply with orders of the presiding officer, or otherwise indicates an intention not to continue the prosecution or defense of an appeal, the presiding officer may issue an order requiring the offending party to show cause why the appeal should not be either dismissed or granted, as appropriate. If the offending party shall fail to show such cause, the presiding officer may issue an Order of Dismissal for failure to prosecute or take such other action deemed reasonable and proper under the circumstances.

Appeal Mailed to BIA Agency Superintendent, Not IBIA; Appellant Bears Consequences of Mis-Mailing Appeal

In the *Estate of Cyprian Buisson*, 53 IBIA 103, 2009, the petition for reconsideration was dismissed as untimely.

> *They did not mail or deliver their petition for reconsideration to the Board, but sent it to the Superintendent of BIA's Standing Rock Agency. The Agency then forwarded the petition to the Board where it was not received until four days after the time for seeking reconsideration had lapsed. Because [they] sent their petition to the wrong entity, they must therefore bear the risk that their appeal would not reach the Board in a timely manner.* (Emphasis added)

The *Estate of Isgrigg Towendolly*, 50 IBIA 206 (09/16/2009), addressed procedural and substantive errors:

> Appellants submitted a Notice of Appeal and an Opening Brief. Their arguments fall into two categories—procedural and substantive.

What Appellants miss is that the alleged procedural defects they cited in Judge Stancampiano's actions were rendered moot by Judge Gordon when, in response to the Petitions for Rehearing, he issued the Notice to all parties to put forth their substantive cases for why another hearing should or should not take place. (Emphasis added)

The IBIA cavalierly dismiss the effect of a possible procedural defect by noting this defect was mooted by the judge giving them a second bite at the apple. There is no accountability by the IBIA.

AIPRA Liability Concerns

Douglas Nash, Director, Institute for Indian Estate Planning and Probate in his Testimony before the Senate Indian Affairs Committee on Backlogs in the Indian Probate System, October 4, 2007, explained some of the liability concerns with AIPRA:

> AIPRA is highly complex with provisions coordinated with other federal acts and codes. The Act, combined with the withdrawal of BIA will drafting services, has created a huge void of specially trained professionals to provide estate planning for Indian people. The need for trained professionals has been voiced to us from every quarter. It is our estimation that there are currently less than 100 legal professionals currently trained nationally. We have already seen the results of will drafting being done by attorneys who are unaware of AIPRA and its ramifications for their clients. This poses a potentially disastrous result for the Indian client in terms of their estate plans and desires. It also poses a potentially disastrous professional liability for the attorney who performed the work.[159] TESTIMONY OF DOUGLAS NASH DIRECTOR, INSTITUTE FOR INDIAN ESTATE PLANNING AND PROBATE SENATE INDIAN AFFAIRS COMMITTEE BACKLOGS IN THE INDIAN PROBATE SYSTEM, October 4, 2007.

> "An imbalance of resources, as well as a reluctance to incur any sort of liability has hindered attempts to fully fund a wide-spread estate-planning approach."[160]

If a will is improperly drafted, it will be set aside and the trust assets will pass intestate.

Indian estate planners must approach tribal trust property with care, Mr. Miller writes:

> It's counterintuitive, but veteran estate-planning lawyers probably commit malpractice more often than others when serving clients who own interests in Native American trust property. Relying on decades of experience with state law, they fail to notice the body of federal Indian law governing will drafting and distribution of trust assets. The most common mistake I see is lawyers attempting to fund a private trust with tribal trust property so their clients can avoid probate. This is critical: You cannot avoid probate for tribal trust assets.[161]

> Also, AIPRA presumes a joint ownership of trust land with a right of survivorship when the owner writes a will that gives a parcel to more than one person. Common law presumes a tenancy in common. … The presumption of joint tenancy means when one of the new owners die, their share automatically goes to the remaining owners. As a result, the last owner living owns all the interests, and the land interests are together again under a single individual. The new rules take this a step further: Anytime the anti-lapse provision conflicts with joint tenancy rule, the joint tenancy wins.[162]

> The federal forum can be especially tricky, even for experienced probate lawyers. For example, the rules of evidence only apply in federal Indian probate hearings to the extent the judge decides they apply.[163]

Probating Individual Indian Trust Property Problems: Locating Heirs and Paternity Determinations

The Indian Land Tenure Foundation states that finding heirs and paternity determinations in probating individual trust property are two definite problem areas. For example, the numbers of IIM account holders without current address information on file with the OST and the unclaimed amounts are staggering. Whereabouts unknown ("WAU") is the term used to describe IIM account holders without current address information on file with the OST.[164]

In 2015, DOI reported that its efforts to locate those on the WAU list had not made a significant dent in the overall number of missing individual beneficiaries.[165] DOI had even gone so far as to hire private investigators at significant cost to locate those with large unclaimed amounts.

Annual amounts in the Whereabouts Unknown Accounts with the number of beneficiaries are briefly set forth below.

2003: Whereabouts Unknown Accounts ("WAU"): 67,716 Accounts totaling $88.5 Million

2008: Whereabouts Unknown Accounts: 85,541 Accounts totaling $73.7 Million

2015: Whereabouts Unknown Accounts: 48,000 Accounts totaling $65 Million

Societal Trends that Will Affect Individual Indian Heirship Determinations: 2021 Center for Disease Control Study Found 68.5% of Births to American Indian and Alaska Native Women Are to Unmarried Women

The numbers from the U.S. Center for Disease Control for the percentage of births to unmarried American Indian and Alaska Native Women are astounding. The trend from 2010 forward is 65%; the rate in 2021 was 68.5%. Unquestionably and indisputably, this trend will impact the determination of heirship. The DOI must factor this into its forward analysis of probate procedures. The upward trend can be seen below:

1970: 22.4%
1980: 39.2%
1990: 53.6%
2000: 58.4%
2010: 65.6%
2021: 68.5%

[Data are based on birth certificates].[166]

Federal Law Applies in Determination of Paternity in Indian Probate Proceedings

For the determination of paternity in Indian probate proceedings 25 U.S.C. § 371 is controlling: it is federal law, not tribal or state law, which controls. *Estate of Joseph Kicking Woman*, 15 IBIA 83 (1987), citing *Estate of Benjamin Kent, Sr.*, 13 IBIA 21 (1984). The statute provides as follows:

25 U.S.C. § 371. Descent of land.

For the purpose of determining the descent of land to the heirs of any deceased Indian under the provisions of the fifth section of said Act, whenever any male and female Indian shall have co-habited together as husband and wife according to the custom and manner of Indian life the issue of such co-habitation shall be, for the purpose aforesaid, taken and deemed to be the legitimate issue of the Indians so living together, and every Indian child, otherwise illegitimate, shall for such purpose be taken and deemed to be the legitimate issue of the father of such child: Provided, That the provisions of this act shall not be held or construed as to apply to the lands commonly called and known as the "Cherokee Outlet". See *Estate of Benjamin Kent, Sr.* (Ben Nawanoway), 13 IBIA 21 (1984).

The *Estate of Wilma Florence First Youngman*, 12 IBIA 219 (1984), explicitly and clearly sets forth the requirement for proving a (1) common-law marriage or (2) an Indian custom marriage … See *Estate of Frances Acres Primeaux Stabler Iron Roubedeaux*, 7 IBIA 254 (1979).

In *Attocknie v. Udall*, 261 F. Supp. 876 (1966); rev'd, 390 F.2d 686 (10th Cir. 1968); cert. denied, 393 U.S. 833 (1968), the Court stated:

The Board [of Indian Appeals] has interpreted [25 U.S.C.] section 371 on numerous occasions. The consistent interpretation has been that the section allows inheritance under two circumstances: (1) when a child is born from an Indian custom marriage, and (2) when the child is illegitimate, but the identity of the father can be proven.

Prong 2 of 25 U.S.C. §371: When Indian Child Is Illegitimate, But Identity of Father Can Be Proven

PHD requires under 25 CFR §15.105, the submittal of documentation useful in establishing paternity:

(c) The place of enrollment and the tribal enrollment or census number of the decedent and potential heirs or devisees;
(e) Any sworn statements regarding the decedent's family, including any statements of paternity or maternity;
(h) Documents from the appropriate authorities, certified if possible, concerning the public record of the decedent, including but not limited to, any:

(1) Marriage licenses and certificates of the decedent;

(3) Adoption and guardianship records concerning the decedent or the decedent's potential heirs or devisees;

(5) Orders requiring payment of child support or spousal support.

At times, the paternity decision is applied to adults who must find the documentation needed to establish paternity after the passage of a significant amount of time. It is a sensitive and private matter.

Federally Approved Tribal Probate Codes

If a tribe has enacted a federally approved tribal probate code, the OHA must follow the tribe's code.

DOI's Tribal Probate Process: In Brief, January 29, 2024

BIA prepares a probate package containing information relating to the person's family history and property holdings for submission to an Administrative Law Judge, Indian Probate Judge, or Attorney Decision Maker (ADM) in the OHA. Each judge has probate jurisdiction over an assigned geographic area.

The probate specialist/clerk completes a probate package that includes:

Evidence of death;

A completed OHA-7 Form: a family tree showing the relatives and indicating which are Indian;

Certified inventory of trust real property;

List of income sources;

All wills, codicils, or repeal of wills;

Debts owed;

Probate specialist/clerk's affidavit that all efforts were made to locate beneficiaries.

The completed package goes to the OHA. While this sounds easy it is not. Again, the problems of heirship determination and paternity are crucial. Given the extensive fractionation of interests over 130 years, it is a *monumental task* to gather and analyze the familial data and the ownership interest(s) of a decedent in trust lands.

An excellent BIA chart documenting this process is available online at: BIA, Your Land Your Decision - What is a Probate? https://www.bia.gov/bia/ots/dop/your-land (accessed online March 14, 2024).

DOI Must Warn Indians to Verify Accuracy and Completeness of Its Probate Data

The DOI's trust responsibility of the "highest moral obligation to Indians" mandates that it *alert* Indians in probate proceedings that it may not rely on the DOI probate case file being complete. (*United States v. Jicarilla Apache Nation*, 564 U.S. 162 (2011)). Similar to *caveat emptor*, it must inform Indians of the difficulties it is incurring in the most basic administrative areas to the more complex trust management protocols. *It is an absolute breach of trust to not forewarn Indians that they cannot rely on the accuracy or completeness of the DOI's data. This must be done conspicuously through Press Releases and online information.*

Next Steps in DOI Probate Process

The judge or ADM conducts a probate hearing at a location convenient for the family members, frequently on the reservation.[167]

The judge or ADM issues an initial decision directing the trust asset distribution among the eligible heirs or devisees. A party who disagrees with the initial decision must seek rehearing from the judge within 30 days from the date of the Decision before appealing to the OHA Interior Board of Indian Appeals.... The BIA Division of Land Titles and Records distributes any trust or restricted land, and the Bureau of Trust Funds Administration (BTFA) distributes trust funds from the deceased person's IIM account to the eligible heirs or devisees listed in OHA's decision.[168]

Timeliness of DOI's Tribal Probate Process

Depending on the complexity of the probate case, DOI's probate process can take several years. In explaining the potentially lengthy time frame, DOI asserts that a probate case is dependent on many factors that are outside of BIA and OHA's control including the cooperation of the family in providing documentation for the probate file. There is no set time frame for the scheduling of hearings, and OHA sometimes returns probate packages to BIA for clarification or further documentation, which can delay the proceedings.[169]

Understaffed, Under-Funded

What Indians facing a probate process today must fully understand in advance, is that the probate landscape has changed. Coordination is required between the BIA, OHA, PHD, OST and the Land Titles and Records Office ("LTRO") building delay into the process.

Douglas Nash's, the Director of the Institute for Indian Estate Planning and Probate which is a project of the Indian Land Tenure Foundation (ILTF), opinion in his 2006 article on AIPRA, expressed his concern that areas such as probate suffer from enough personnel to provide services and the ever-pressing need to reduce workload and costs.[170] It is an ongoing concern that cannot be buried away. A probate specialist/clerk only has so much time it can dedicate to completing a probate package. The BIA reported it is having difficulties hiring personnel due to their fear of liability if their work is challenged, especially since they must prepare an affidavit that all efforts were made to locate beneficiaries.

Lack of Functioning Communication Equipment

Even in 2024, the cost-pressures are evident from several OHA and PHD offices not having full communication established. The Albuquerque, New Mexico, PHD Field Office was serving as a central conduit for facsimile and telephone call responses to several other PHD Field Offices. As instructed by the OHA Sacramento Field Office and the OHA Director's Office in Arlington, Virginia, communication to the (1) Sacramento OHA Office and (2) Arlington, VA OHA Director's office, was being routed through the Albuquerque PHD. The (1) Sacramento OHA Office and (2) Arlington, VA Director's offices' facsimile machines were not operational.

Hiring New Legal Assistants

In 2024, the ABQ PHD Office in 2024 stated that communication was also difficult due to new legal assistants assuming their positions.

9: Legal Defects in 2024
Individual Indian Probate Case Decision

Legal Defects in 2024 Individual Indian Probate Case Decision re Heirship Determination and Co-Owners' Option to Purchase Decedent's Interest in Restricted Trust Property

Dates Were Not Stated

Dates by which actions would be taken were unstated, creating confusion.

Failure to Include Family Members of which BIA and OHA Had Been Given Written Notice and Confirmed as Received

In a recent individual Indian probate case ("Indian Probate Case"), the *BIA acknowledged in writing that the Decedent's half-siblings constituted Interested Parties* and should be designated as such, but it would be up to the Indian Probate Judge assigned the Case. Yet they were not identified as "actual or potential heirs" and have never been afforded this designation ("Omitted Parties"). While they are far down on the chain of inheritance, they are "actual or potential heirs" based on qualification as Indian half-siblings.

This information is known to the BIA which routinely gathers familial information and information pertaining to ownership of trust properties.

In coordination with the Division of Probate Services ("DPS"), BIA's data makes it possible for the DPS to compile inventories of Indian Trust assets and family information, and to coordinate the timely distribution of trust assets with the Office of Hearings and Appeals ("OHA"), the Division of Land Titles and Records ("DLTR"), and the Bureau of Trust Funds Administration ("BTFA").[171]

Douglas Nash Director, Institute for Indian Estate Planning and Probate in his testimony before the Senate Indian Affairs Committee on Backlogs in the Indian Probate System, October 4, 2007, stated:

> Changes in ownership are not necessarily recorded at a uniform pace and a probate file may be sent forward that does not include all of the interests owned by a decedent at the time of death, making the probate inaccurate and necessitating additional probate proceedings and a modification of a final probate order. When a final probate order is issued, that order is sent to back to the BIA where changes in title ownership—from the decedent to heirs—is to be recorded.

> There are errors in the land title records. ...

> Outdated ownership records and databases create a new probate backlog as they are corrected, increasing the work for the BIA and OHA.

Failure to Include Omitted Parties as "Interested Parties" and Afford Them Legal Rights

In the Indian Probate Case, the Omitted Parties who fall under the Definition of "Interested party," under 43 CFR Part 30, Subpart A §30.101, were not designated as such. Under AIPRA "Interested party means: (1) Any potential or actual heir; (2) Any devisee under a will; (3) Any person or entity asserting a claim against a decedent's estate; (4) Any tribe having a statutory option to purchase the trust or restricted property interest of a decedent; or (5) Any co-owner exercising a purchase option." The Omitted Parties fall under categories 1 and 5.

Failure to Include Co-Owners in Trust Restricted Property of which BIA and OHA Had Been Given Written Notice and Confirmed as Received

In the Indian Probate Case, the Decedent's co-owners in the Restricted Trust Property were not made parties to the Indian Probate Case. Again, *the BIA and OHA PHD had been repeatedly alerted in writing, confirmed as received, that the Omitted Parties were co-owners in the Decedent's Restricted Trust Property.*

Judge Kienzle in his ORDER GRANTING IN PART PETITION FOR REOPENING AND ORDER TO SHOW CAUSE TO HEIRS ("Partial Reopening Order") stated:

The BIA did not provide any confirmation in the record regarding the co-owners of Allotment _____. This tribunal's review of records contained in the Department's records indicates that [the Omitted Parties] are co-owners of that property.

Failure to Consider Co-Owners' Option to Purchase Decedent's Restricted Property of which BIA and OHA Had Been Given Written Notice and Confirmed as Received

If you pass away without a will, one of your heirs, co-owners or the tribe may petition the probate court to purchase your interests in trust or restricted land. If the undivided interest is 5% or more, consent must be obtained by the potential purchaser before any sale can go through. On the other hand, an undivided interest of less than 5% may be sold without the consent of your heir (unless the heir or spouse is living on the parcel where interest is located). The purchase price must be at least the fair market value and the payment distributed to your heirs after the sale.[172]

In the Indian Probate Case, *the BIA and OHA PHD had been repeatedly alerted in writing, confirmed as received, as to the co-owners' decision to* exercise their option to purchase Decedent's estate under AIPRA. Judge Kienzle acknowledged in the Partial Reopening Order that: "*The Decision did not address the request to purchase at probate.*" He further acknowledged in the Partial Reopening Order that: "*If a request to purchase is filed before the completion of the first probate hearing, the request should be addressed in the Decision. [Omitted Parties'] request to purchase Decedent's interest in Allotment___was not addressed in the Decision.*" (Emphasis added)

If Judge Kienzle had not issued the Partial Reopening Order, the co-owners would have been precluded from exercising their option to purchase Decedent's estate under AIPRA.

The Presiding Judge *merely noted these failures* in the Indian Probate Case. They resulted in the Omitted Parties having to request a petition for reopening from the Presiding Judge or the BIA and "showing cause" why they were entitled to a reopening of the closed probate case.

Failure to Conduct Formal Probate Given Restricted Trust Property Is Part of Decedent's Estate of which BIA and OHA Had Been Given Written Notice and Confirmed as Received

No distinction was made in the Indian Probate Case whether the proceeding was formal or summary. The ABQ PHD thought it was a summary proceeding.

Failure to Give Notice to Omitted Parties of Commencement of Probate Proceedings in Indian Probate Case

Under 43 CFR Part 30, Subpart J Formal Probate Proceedings §§30.114 and 30.210, notice to Interested Parties must be given, permitting their participation in the case. This did not occur in the Indian Probate Case which qualified for Formal Probate Proceedings since it included restricted trust property.

Judge Kienzle acknowledged in the Partial Reopening Order that: "The probate hearing was held on _____. A Notice of that hearing was mailed on _____. *Notice of that hearing was not provided to [Omitted Parties]*." (Emphasis added)

Again, this was a mere aside for the Presiding Judge. While it is advisable to specifically request notice to the BIA and OHA Offices assigned the Indian Probate Case, *this will absolutely not assure notice is given. The BIA and OHA PHD had been repeatedly requested to provide notice to the Omitted Parties. The OHA PHD emailed the following notice, to the parties who were omitted, in advance of the hearing in the Indian Probate Case:*

> *We will add you and ___ and ___ as interested parties to this matter so that you will be informed of the hearing date, once one is set. The Judge, once assigned, will hold a hearing to determine who Decedent's heirs are. Any further questions raised in your letter can be addressed with the Judge at the hearing.* (Emphasis added)

No notice was given Omitted Parties of the (1) initiation of the probate proceedings in the Indian Probate Case; (2) Indian Probate Case hearing in the Case; (3) Indian Probate Case Notice of Decision and Decision in the Case, or (4) any other notice required in a BIA/OHA probate proceeding.

Failure to Represent if Requisite Federal Indian Paternity Determination Was Made

In the Indian Probate Case, *the BIA and OHA PHD had been repeatedly alerted in writing, confirmed as received, as to the need for a paternity determination.* Judge Kienzle's Decision merely stated the following: "As of the date of death the Decedent was unmarried and his closest surviving relatives were his four children."

There was no discussion, expression, findings, and/or conclusions as to the basis for determination of paternity.

Violation of U.S. Constitution, Statutory Law, Agency Regulations and Procedures, and Interior Board of Indian Appeals ("IBIA") Decisions

A Decision that does not constitute the foregoing requisites constitutes a violation of the rights of the Omitted Parties under: (1) the Administrative Procedure Act which requires reviewing courts to invalidate agency actions found to be "arbitrary, capricious, an abuse of discretion, or otherwise not in accordance with law"; (2) due process of law requirements under the Fifth Amendment to the U.S. Constitution which provides that no person "shall be deprived of life, liberty, or property, without due process of law"; (3) AIPRA; (4) the OHA's and BIA's probate regulations and procedures; and (5) IBIA Decisions.

Conflicting Instructions

In conflicting instructions, Judge John R. Payne, issued a NOTICE OF PETITION FOR REOPENING, with all communication to be directed to Indian Probate Judge Kienzle.

The BIA Superintendent, though, directed Counsel, via email, as follows:

> The individuals that are requesting an appeal will need to contact the Office of Hearings and Appeals, located in Billings, MT and their contact number is 406-657-6960. Appeal documentation can also be sent to the Office of Hearings and Appeals' address: 2900 4th Ave. N #301, Billings, MT 59101.

Petitioners were not requesting an appeal and without a designation as Interested Parties lacked any appeal rights.

Petitioning for Reopening of Closed Case Is Back-End Approach

Petitioning for the Reopening of a Closed Case when you have been wrongfully omitted from the probate proceeding is not due process. The IBIA merely stating that the alleged procedural defects in a case are rendered moot by the subsequent action of a judge in a response to the Petition for Rehearing, does not rectify the damage done. The majority of allottees don't have the resources to pursue this avenue or may not even know trust lands they have an interest in are being or have been probated if they have been excluded from any notice of probate.

It reminds me of an exchange between Congressional representatives on the floor of the House in 1884 when they were debating the cession of all 3,000,000 acres of the Red Lake Band lands to afford the people of Northwestern Minnesota an opportunity to avail themselves of the pine timber on the reservation and opening "up a large area to thrifty, energetic settlers all over the land." According to the Committee, the reservation "occupied by less than 1,200 semi-civilized Chippewa Indians ... is of little use or benefit to the Indians."[173]

The congressional debate on the bill introduced for the cession of the land vilified Indians in a most racist and degrading manner. Representative Joseph McCrum Belford of New York led the charge. His description of the Cherokee removal, which generated laughter in Congress reminds me of the back-end approach:

> Yes, my dear friend from Arkansas, do you recollect how they dragged those poor Indians out of the State of Georgia? Why, sir, they absolutely tied them to the tails of their horses. [Laughter.][174]

This was followed by an ignominious reply from Representative Poindexter Dunn of Arkansas:

> I will give my friend the benefit of a story my father's servant, Dick, told him. He said that the first impression he had of the Indians was what he saw of them on their move from Georgia to the Territory, and that every Indian was part man and part horse for they were all tied together. [Laughter.][175]

Due Process and Meaningful Opportunity to Be Heard

The Due Process Clause under the Fifth Amendment to the U.S. Constitution is essentially a guarantee of basic fairness. Fairness can, in various cases, have many components: notice, an opportunity to be heard at a meaningful time in a meaningful way, and a decision supported by substantial evidence. Reopening the Probate Case as a back-end measure does not afford due process of law and a meaningful opportunity to be heard in determining heirship and consideration of an option to purchase Decedent's estate.

How to Get Notice of Federal Indian Probate Hearings

The new regulations require OHA to post notice of upcoming hearings on its website and by physical postings.[176] This is acceptable if you know a case is coming up for hearing or if you live on the reservation where the Decedent did or where the restricted trust property is located. This does not excuse the personal notice by OHA to Interested Parties in a Formal Probate proceeding.

Reopening Closed Indian Probate Cases

Under 43 CFR Part 30, Subpart J §30.243, the BIA or an interested party may file a petition for reopening a closed probate case or the judge may act sua sponte (on his own accord).

> § 30.243 May a closed probate case be reopened?
> A closed probate case may be reopened if the decision or order issued in the probate case contains an error of fact or law (including, but not limited to, a missing or improperly included heir or devisee, a found will, or an error in the distribution of property), and the error is discovered more than 30 days after the mailing date of a decision.
> (a) Any *interested party or BIA* may seek correction of the error of fact or law by filing a petition for reopening with the judge. (Emphasis added)
> (b) Reopening may also be initiated on a judge's own motion.

Since Judge Kienzle had not designated the Omitted Parties as Interested Parties they had no basis to petition for reopening the case. Also, since they did not know of the Decision rendered by Judge Kienzle, until more than 30 days after it occured, they missed the deadline in the Decision.

IBIA Decisions Standard of Manifest Injustice Changed to Balancing Test in New Rules for Reopening Closed Indian Probate Cases

The following information is directly from the DOI's Website, Rehearings and Reopening Estates:

> The BIA may seek reopening of an estate to correct manifest error. *Estate of John Yazza Antonio*, 12 IBIA 177 (1984); *Estate of Paul Widow*, 17 IBIA 107 (1989). The Board has held that the BIA has a responsibility to seek reopening when it has information indicating some likelihood that a probate decision is incorrect and that it is manifest injustice for the BIA to have such information and not act on it. *Estate of Paul Widow*, 17 IBIA 107 (1989).

> The new regulations replace the manifest injustice standard with a balancing test. The test considers whether the "need to correct the error outweighs the

interests of the public and heirs or devisees in the finality of the probate proceeding[.]"

The regulations, found at 43 C.F.R. § 30.243 - § 30.249, provide eight factors to help judges decide whether to grant reopening: 1) the nature of the error, 2) the passage of time, 3) whether the petitioner exercised due diligence in pursuing their rights, 4) whether the petitioner's ancestor exercised due diligence in pursuing their rights and whether a failure to exercise should be imputed to the petitioner, 5) the availability of witnesses and documents, 6) finality, 7) the number of estates that would be affected by the reopening, and 8) whether the property that was in the estate is still available for redistribution.

Counsel for Omitted Parties Contacted BIA and OHA Officials Petitioning for Reopening Indian Probate Case

A Petition for Reopening was submitted to the BIA and the OHA. The BIA advised Counsel to file an Appeal and advised Counsel that the Case was before OHA and provided an address and telephone number. The problem was the time period for filing an appeal from Judge Kienzle's Decision had passed. The Omitted Parties were unaware that a Decision had been rendered until after the 30-day appeal period had expired. Counsel learned of the Decision when it contacted the OHA for an update on the case. The only legal option was to petition for the BIA or Judge Kienzle to reopen the closed probate case.

Wrong Addresses on OHA Website

The Petition for Reopening was mailed Certified Mail, Return Receipt Requested to (1) Judge Kienzle; (2) the Supervisory Indian Probate Judge, OHA, Field Office; and (3) the Paralegal Specialist, OHA Field Office, and (4) other parties in the BIA and the OHA. The addresses listed on the OHA website were used. Each of the letters mailing the Petition to the Presiding Judge; (2) Supervisory Indian Probate Judge, OHA, Field Office; and (3) Paralegal Specialist, OHA Field Office with jurisdiction over the Probate Case were all returned to Counsel as undeliverable. The U.S. Post Office stated the following on the three letters which were all returned to Counsel: "RETURN TO SENDER NOT DELIVERABLE AS ADDRESSED UNABLE TO FORWARD."

The warning in this instance: Do not rely on the website information. Use the letterhead address information as instructed, in this case, by the OHA.

The Petition for Reopening was mailed to all of the parties to get their attention to the mistakes made in the Indian Probate Case. The Presiding Judge objected to this even though the Omitted Parties had not been given any legal status whatsoever, other than appearing on a mailing list to "parties or entities" by the ALJ.

Chief Administrative Law Judge Sent Parties Copies of a Notice of Petition for Reopening to BIA and Assigned Case to Indian Probate Judge Kienzle (Judge Kienzle or "Presiding Judge" or "IPJ")

The Notice of Petition for Reopening stated:

> TO: Superintendent, _____ Agency
> Pursuant to 43 C.F.R. § 30.243, please take notice that a petition for reopening has been filed in this proceeding. Any further payment of claims and distribution of this estate is stayed while the petition for reopening remains pending, unless otherwise directed. Judge Kienzle has been assigned to this case and all filings in these proceedings should be filed with him at the Rapid City office at the above address.

Sua Sponte Reopening of Indian Probate Case by Judge

The judge who decided an Indian Probate Case has the authority to reopen it (43 CFR Part 30, Subpart C §30.129) on his own motion or petition by an Interested Party. Though the Notice of Petition for Reopening from Judge Kienzle's supervisor did not state it had been reopened, that is what occurred.

Partial Reopening Order by Judge Kienzle

Judge Kienzle did not inform the Omitted Parties that he had reopened the Indian Probate Case, even though 43 CFR Part 30, Subpart C §30.129(b), requires the judge to notify Interested Parties if a case is reopened and to "conduct appropriate proceedings." They found out when they received his Partial Reopening Order. Again, neither the Omitted Parties nor Counsel were afforded an opportunity to participate or to be heard which is 'permitted' under the new rules. According to one of OHA's paralegals, the judge unilaterally reviews the case to determine if it was lawfully handled by him/her, with a proper legal decision rendered. The Partial Reopening Order affirmed the heirship based on Judge Kienzle's review of South Dakota Birth Certificates and *included the required language regarding the Omitted Parties right to exercise an option to purchase the Decedent's interest.*

Judge Kienzle's Partial Reopening Order Confusing: States Co-Owners of Allotment Have Standing to Seek Reopening of Decision in Indian Probate Case and Petition for Reopening is Appropriate Process at This Stage When It Would Appear Indian Probate Case Already Reopened

The Partial Reopening Order states: If [Omitted Parties] are co-owners of Allotment ___, they have standing to seek reopening of the Decision. The Partial Reopening Order further stated: The tribunal reminds [Counsel] that a petition for reopening is the appropriate process to use when challenging the Decision at this stage. *Yet it appeared the IPJ had already sua sponte reopened the Case. The Omitted Parties requested clarification from the IPJ of the foregoing statements, as well as an Order designating them as Interested Parties to assure standing to appeal to the IBIA.*

OHA's Advice to File FOIA to Get Indian Probate Case File

According to OHA, the only way for the Omitted Parties to secure access to the Probate Case File was to file a FOIA. OHA further represented that DOI's processing of a FOIA request would take a substantial amount of time, as would a case reopening determination. In addition, the information regarding heirship has been designated as confidential under "Interior BIA-27: BIA Probate Files" which may make it more difficult, if not impossible, to access.

Notice of Entry of Appearance in Case Parties Want to Sell their Interests

Counsel filed a Notice of Entry of Appearance in case the parties identified for distribution of the Restricted Trust Property wanted to sell their interests and Counsel would then have a role in the Indian Probate Case.

Indian Will-Drafting Services

Many non-profit organizations and law schools are providing Indian will-drafting services, not necessarily by attorneys, but law school students and other trained professionals. AIPRA authorizes DOI to provide noncompetitive grants to tribes, organizations that provide legal assistance services, and others to conduct estate planning services for tribes and assist individual Indians. 22 U.S.C. §2206(f)(3).

POSTSCRIPT

Need for Concrete Determination and Announcement by BIA as to What Law Controls in Determining Paternity in Intestate AIPRA Cases

As the AIPRA was enacted to apply federal, not state law, if the OHA disingenuously applies state law, it is an assault on tribal sovereignty. It would mean OHA, a trustee, a fiduciary in the realm of probate of Indian estates, may wantonly ignore Congress' mandate that federal law applies, not state law, within the boundaries of Indian reservations on trust lands. According to one BIA Superintendent, federal, not state law, applies. Also, the IBIA similarly stated that they were nailing down the coffin lid on what law applies in *Indian probate paternity determinations, and it is federal law that applies.*

> *To the extent the Board's prior cases may not have nailed down the coffin lid on the question of whether state law, including state law evidentiary standards, apply in, it does so now.* Estate of Richard Crawford, 42 IBIA 64 (2005). (Emphasis added)

> The AIPRA provides a probate process for trust assets of American Indians. … *Prior to the enactment of AIPRA, the probate of trust assets was governed by the state law where the trust or restricted land was located. See* https://www.bia.gov/bia/ots/dps/approved-tribal-probate-codes (accessed online March 5, 2024).

February 2024: "Order Granting in Part Petition for Reopening and Order to Show Cause to Heirs"

Judge Kienzle stated he relied on state law (S.D. Codified Laws § 34-25-13.2) and the IBIA's 1995 case that state law was applicable in determining paternity in an intestate AIPRA Indian probate case:

I found that the evidence in the record is sufficient to show that Decedent is the father of the four children. ... Birth certificates for each child, issued by the State of South Dakota, are included in the record. Decedent is identified as the father of each of the 4 children on the birth certificates. *A father's name listed on a birth certificate is documentary evidence of paternity. Estate of William Youpee, 28 IBIA 200, 202 (1995). Further, under South Dakota law, if the mother of a child is not married at the time of conception or birth, the father's name may not be included on the birth certificate without written consent of the mother and purported father or a judicial determination of paternity. S.D. Codified Laws § 34-25-13.2. Thus, the birth certificates are very reliable evidence that Decedent is the father of the children.* (Emphasis added)

April 2024: "Order Denying in Part Petition for Reopening and Denying Request to Purchase at Probate"

Judge Kienzle appeared to state that there is no basis for arguing federal law applies in AIPRA intestate cases.

> _____ argued that state law does not apply to the probate of federal Indian trust property. *The reason for her argument on that issue is unclear.* Presumably, she was arguing that the determination that Decedent was the father of the 4 children who were determined to be his heirs should not be based on state law. However, that determination was not based on state law. It was based on the highly reliable evidence contained in the record. (Emphasis added)

Judge Kienzle stated that he did not rely on state law, but on highly reliable evidence contained in the record without any further information as to what that evidence was. This is contrary to what he stated in his prior response in February 2024.

BIA Should Also Come Up with Process to Provide Access to Probate Case File other than Filing Freedom of Information Act Request

The BIA should also come up with a process to provide access to the probate case file in an AIPRA case, other than the respondent filing a Freedom of Information Act ("FOIA") request. Judge Kienzle's response to a repeated request for access to the probate case is as follows:

> The BIA is the official custodian of the record. _____ may file a Freedom

of Information Act request to the _____ [BIA] Agency seeking a copy of the probate file.

This is in accord with the OHA's advice:

> According to OHA, the only way for the Omitted Parties to secure access to the Probate Case File was to file a FOIA. *OHA further represented that DOI's processing of a FOIA request would take a substantial amount of time*, as would a case reopening determination. (Emphasis added)

Getting Copy of Indian Probate Case File

As stated by the Stewards of Indigenous Resources Endowment, December 20, 2019, in its Comments on DOI-2019-0001, Updates to American Indian Probate Regulations:

> Interested parties rarely see their federal probate case files. Before AIPRA, it was unclear whether parties had a right to view their files at all. Today, they are able to request the files if they do so in writing, although most probably do not know this. When files are requested, they sometimes arrive long after the initial hearing. *A system more devoted to due process would guarantee that a copy of the file is delivered to each interested party along with the notice of initial hearing*. (Emphasis added)

Also as stated by Attorney Jared Miller, getting a copy of the probate file is CRITICAL to preparing a case:

Per Mr. Miller:

> What's the first thing you do after agreeing to represent a party in a federal Indian probate case? You request a copy of the probate file from the Office of Hearings and Appeals (OHA). Even then, the file probably won't arrive in time for the initial hearing; you might go in blind.
>
> Then you'll have to convince the judge to set a supplemental hearing and hope the file arrives before then. Judge's like to probate estates at the initial hearing if possible, so come prepared with a good reason to delay.
>
> Once you get the file, you can prepare your case.
> (https://www.indianprobatelawyer.com/blog (accessed online March 14, 2024.))

Problem with Filing a FOIA Request

Information regarding heirship may be designated as confidential under "Interior BIA-27: BIA Probate Files" which may make it more difficult, if not impossible, to access under a FOIA request. Again, the BIA should come up with a process to provide access to the probate case file in an AIPRA case, other than the respondent filing a FOIA request.

NOTES

1. Address by General Pope before the Social Science Association, at Cincinnati, Ohio, May 24, 1878. Delivered by Request of the Association (Cincinnati: n.p., 1878). Excerpt From: Editor, Cozzens, Peter. "Eyewitnesses to the Indian Wars: 1865-1890: Vol.5, The Army and the Indian." Apple Books.

2. Dealing with the whip end of someone else's crazy: individual-based approaches to Indian land fractionation, South Dakota Law Review, Vol. 57, No. 2, June 2012.

3. https://www.thefreelibrary.com/Dealing+with+the+whip+end+of+someone+else%27s+crazy%3A+individual-based...-a0320732073 (accessed online March 14, 2024).

4. https://www.ndstudies.gov/curriculum/high-school/standing-rock-oyate/documents-standing-rock (accessed online April 9, 2023).

5. Inheriting Indian Land Fact Sheets, Montana State University, Fact Sheet 14 - Definitions.

6. Inheriting Indian Land Fact Sheets, Montana State University, Fact Sheet #1 What is AIPRA and how does it affect you?

7. Inheriting Indian Land Fact Sheets, Montana State University Fact Sheet #6: Your undivided interests of 5% or more: What happens if you pass away without a written will?

8. Jared Miller, Apr. 22, 2023, Native Americans rarely represented by counsel in BIA probates. https://www.indianprobatelawyer.com/blog (accessed online March 14, 2024). Stewards of Indigenous Resources Endowment, December 20, 2019, Comments on DOI-2019-0001, Updates to American Indian Probate Regulations.

9. https://www.thefreelibrary.com/Dealing+with+the+whip+end+of+someone+else%27s+crazy%3A+individual-based...-a0320732073 (accessed online March 21, 2024).

10. Jared Miller. https://www.indianprobatelawyer.com/blog (accessed online March 14, 2024).

11. Letter from Secretary of the Interior Z. Chandler to Secretary of War Belknap, December 3, 1875, U.S., Congress, House, Military Expedition

Against the Sioux Indians, 44 Cong. 1 sess. 1876, H. Ex. Doc. 184, p. 10.

12. Doane Robinson, History of the Sioux, op. cit., p. 422.

13. Letter of Indian Commissioner J. Q. Smith to Secretary of Interior Z. Chandler, l44 Cong. 1 sess. V. XIV, (ser 1691), H. EX. DOC. 184, p. 18.

14. U.S., Congress, House, Military Expedition Against the Sioux Indians, 44th Cong., 1st Sess., 1876, House Ex. Doc. 184, p. 10.

15. https://www.law.cornell.edu/wex/order_to_show_cause (accessed online March 21, 2024).

16. Comments on DOI-2019-0001, Updates to American Indian Probate Regulations.

17. https://www.americanbar.org/groups/crsj/publications/human_rights_magazine_home/wealth-disparities-in-civil-rights/federal-policies-trap-tribes-in-poverty/#:~:text=More%20than%20one%20in%20four,who%20reside%20within%20Indian%20Country (accessed online March 14, 2024).

18. David J. Wishart. An Unspeakable Sadness: The Dispossession of the Nebraska Indians. University of Nebraska Press, 1994, p. 55.

19. https://www.ndstudies.gov/curriculum/high-school/standing-rock-oyate/documents-standing-rock (accessed online April 9, 2023).

20. http://savagesandscoundrels.org/people/savages-scoundrels/chief-old-dog/ (accessed online November 20, 2020).

21. Story, Joseph. 1 Commentaries on the Constitution of the United States. §3 (1st ed. 1833).

22. The Land Act of 1820 Act of April 24 1820. 3 Stat. 566 (accessed online November 2, 2023).

23. Blegen, Theodore C. Minnesota: A History of the State. University of Minnesota Press, 1975: 322.

24. Schlebecker, John T. Whereby We Thrive: A History of American Farming, 1607–1972. Iowa State University Press, 1975: 62.

25. https://www.raremaps.com/gallery/detail/34312/a-new-map-of-the-western-parts-of-virginia-pennsylvania-ma-hutchins (accessed online November 8, 2020).

26. "From John Adams to Cherokee Nation, 27 August 1798," Founders Online, National Archives. https://founders.archives.gov/documents/Adams/99-02-02-2892 (accessed online November 13, 2020).

27. "From Thomas Jefferson to John Breckinridge, 12 August 1803," Founders Online, National Archives. https://founders.archives.gov/documents/Jefferson/01-41-02-0139. [Original source: The Papers of Thomas Jefferson, vol. 41, 11 July–15 November 1803, ed. Barbara B. Oberg. Princeton: Princeton University Press, 2014, pp. 184–186.] (accessed online November 13, 2020).

28. "From Thomas Jefferson to George Rogers Clark, 25 December 1780,"

Founders Online, National Archives. https://founders.archives.gov/documents/Jefferson/01-04-02-0295. [Original source: The Papers of Thomas Jefferson, vol. 4, 1 October 1780 – 24 February 1781, ed. Julian P. Boyd. Princeton: Princeton University Press, 1951, pp. 233–238.] (accessed online November 13, 2020).

29. "From James Madison to United States Congress, 3 December 1816," Founders Online, National Archives. https://founders.archives.gov/documents/Madison/99-01-02-5598 (accessed online November 4, 2020).

30. James Monroe, First Annual Message Online by Gerhard Peters and John T. Woolley, The American Presidency Project. https://www.presidency.ucsb.edu/node/205560 (accessed online November 4, 2020).

31. Second Inaugural Address of James Monroe, March 5, 1821. https://avalon.law.yale.edu/19th_century/monroe2.asp (accessed online November 14, 2020).

32. President James Monroe, in an 1825 message to Congress in Native American Voices: A History and Anthology, ed. Steven Mintz (St. James, New York: Brandywine P, 1995), 111-112.

33. John C. Calhoun to James Monroe, February 8, 1822, ASP: Indian Affairs, 2: 275-6.

34. Andrew Jackson to James Monroe, March 4, 1817, Jackson Papers, 4: 93-98.

35. Banner, Stuart. How the Indians lost their land: Law and power on the frontier. Harvard University Press, 2005: 199.

36. James Barbour to John Crowell, January 29, 1827; Barbour to Troup, January 29, 1827; Barbour to John H. Morel, January 30, 1827; Barbour to R. W. Habersham, January 30, 1827; Barbour to Lieutenant J. R. Vinton, January 30, 1827, ASP: Indian Affairs, 2: 864-5. James Barbour to John Crowell, January 31, 1827, M21 3: 349.

37. February 5, 1827: Message Regarding the Creek Indians. https://millercenter.org/the-presidency/presidential-speeches/february-5-1827-message-regarding-creek-indians (accessed online November 4, 2020).

38. Id.

39. Relinquishment of the Claims of the Creeks to the Lands in Georgia, American State Papers: Indian Affairs, 2: 871.

40. Banner, Stuart. How the Indians lost their land: Law and power on the frontier. Harvard University Press, 2005: 208.

41. Id.

42. Georgia's Notorious Yazoo Land Fraud And Its Consequences, Part 2. https://georgelamplugh.com/2018/01/01/georgias-notorious-yazoo-land-fraud-and-its-consequences-part-2-in-pursuit-of-dead-georgians-27/#:~:text=A%20more%20tragic%20legacy%20of,claims%20of%20the%20Creeks%20and (accessed online March 22, 2024).

43. President Jackson's Message to Congress "On Indian Removal", December 6, 1830; Records of the United States Senate, 1789-1990; Record Group 46;

Records of the United States Senate, 1789-1990; National Archives and Records Administration (NARA).

44. Green, Michael D. *The politics of Indian removal: Creek government and society in crisis.* U of Nebraska Press, 1982: 69-14; "Creek Indians," Niles' Weekly Register 22 (1824): 223; U.S. Commissioners to Creek Chiefs, 9 December 1824, Document TCC008, SNA.

45. Foster, Arthur. *A Digest of the Laws of the State of Georgia: Containing All Statutes, and the Substance of All Resolutions of a General and Public Nature, and Now in Force, which Have Been Passed in Said State from the Year 1820 to the Year 1829 Inclusive: with Occasional Explanatory Notes and Connecting References, and a List of the Statutes Repealed Or Obsolete to which is Added an Appendix, Containing the Constitution of the State of Georgia, as Amended, Also References to Such Local Acts as Relate to Towns ....* Towar, J. & D.M. Hogan, 1831: 126-129.

46. Niles' Weekly Register, December 19, 1829.

47. Letter from General John Coffee to Secretary of War Eaton, October 14, 1829.

48. Documents and Proceedings Relating to the Formation and Progress of a Board in the City of New York, for the Emigration, Preservation, and Improvement, of the Aborigines of North America. (New York: Vanderpool and Cole, 1829), pp. 21-22.

49. Id.

50. Alfred Balch to Andrew Jackson, January 8, 1830; Andrew Jackson Papers: Series 1, General Correspondence and Related Items, 1775-1885 (15,697).

51. S. 102. Bills and Resolutions, Senate, 21st Cong., 1st Sess., February 22, 1830.

52. James D. Richardson, Messages and Papers of the Presidents, Vol. 2, 456-9.

53. https://www.wcu.edu/library/DigitalCollections/CherokeePhoenix/Vol3/no13/from-the-arkansas-gazette-page-2-column-1a.html (accessed online March 22, 2024).

54. https://www.wcu.edu/library/DigitalCollections/CherokeePhoenix/Vol3/no25/this-issue-of-the-phoenix-is-published-in-four-columns-only-page-1-column-1a-page-3-column-1a.html (accessed online December 13, 2020).

55. Speech of Mr. Frelinghuysen, of New Jersey, delivered in the Senate of the United States, April 6, 1830, on The Bill For An Exchange Of Lands With The Indians Residing In Any Of The States Or Territories And For Their Removal West Of The Mississippi.

56. Ibid., p. 10.

57. Ibid., p. 22.

58. Ibid., p. 5.

59. Speech of Mr. Sprague, of Maine: Delivered in the Senate of the United States, 16th April, 1830, in Reply to Messrs. White, McKinley, and Forsyth,

upon the Subject of the Removal of the Indians. Published at the Office of the National Journal, Peter Force, 1830: 40.

60. United States. Congress. Speeches on the Passage of the Bill for the Removal of the Indians, Delivered in the Congress of the United States, April and May, 1830, Perkins and Marvin, 1830: 76.

61. Ibid., 112.

62. Id.

63. Ibid., 119.

64. Rives, John Cook, et al. The Congressional Globe. United States, Blair & Rives: 1559.

65. United States. Congress. Speeches of the Passage of the Bill for the Removal of the Indians, Delivered in the Congress of the United States, April and May, 1830, Perkins and Marvin, 1830.

66. Ibid, 299.

67. Ibid., 253.

68. Lamar Marshall, Larry Smith, Michael Wren. Alabama Collection Camps, Forts, Emigrating Depots and Travel Routes Used During the Cherokee Removal of 1838-1839. https://www.nps.gov/trte/learn/historyculture/upload/Alabama-Collections-Camps-Forts-Depots-and-Routes-508.pdf (accessed online November 29, 2020).

69. de Tocqueville, Alexis. Democracy in America. Vol. I & II. Regnery Publishing, 2003: 346.

70. https://www.bia.gov/faqs/what-federal-indian-reservation (accessed online September 1, 2022).

71. Report of the Commissioner of Indian Affairs to the Secretary of the Interior, Office of Indian Affairs, United States. 1872, pp. 5-6.

72. Report of the Commissioner of Indian Affairs to the Secretary of the Interior, United States. Office of Indian Affairs. U.S. Government Printing Office, 1868, Extract, p. I.

73. Annual Report of the Commissioner of Indian Affairs to the Secretary of the Interior. United States. Office of Indian Affairs, U.S. Government Printing Office, 1877, p. 10. Report of the Commissioner of Indian Affairs to the Secretary of the Interior, United States. Office of Indian Affairs. U.S. Government Printing Office, 1877, p. 151.

74. Report of the Commissioner of Indian Affairs to the Secretary of the Interior, United States. Office of Indian Affairs. U.S. Government Printing Office, 1890, p. V.

75. Maura Grogan, "Native American Lands and Natural Resource Development," Revenue Watch Institute, NY, NY, 2011, pp. 3, 6, 10, 11.

76. Annual Report of the Board of Indian Commissioners (Washington, 1869), pp. 5-11.

77. Report of the Commissioner of Indian Affairs to the Secretary of the Interior, United States. Office of Indian Affairs. U.S. Government Printing Office, 1872, pp. 9-10.

78. Report of the Commissioner of Indian Affairs to the Secretary of the Interior. United States. Office of Indian Affairs. U.S. Government Printing Office, 1876, p. VI.

79. Report of Special Agent Edwin Brooks to Commissioner of Indian Affairs.

80. Report of the Commissioner of Indian Affairs to the Secretary of the Interior. United States. Office of Indian Affairs. U.S. Government Printing Office, 1878, p. VIII.

81. General Allotment Act, ch. 119, § 5, 24 Stat. 388, 389 (1887) (codified at 25 U.S.C. § 331 (1988).

82. Burke Act, ch. 2348, 34 Stat. 182, 183 (1906) (current version at 25 U.S.C. § 349 (2006).

83. Nash, Douglas R. and Burke, Cecelia E. (2006) "The Changing Landscape of Indian Estate Planning and Probate: The American Indian Probate Reform Act (AIPRA)," Seattle Journal for Social Justice: Vol. 5: Iss. 1, Article 15, p. 126. https://digitalcommons.law.seattleu.edu/sjsj/vol5/iss1/15 (accessed online March 15, 2024).

84. Report of the Commissioner of Indian Affairs to the Secretary of the Interior. United States. Office of Indian Affairs. U.S. Government Printing Office, 1885, p. V.

85. H. Rept. No. 1576, vol. V (H. R. 5038), May 28, 1880, p. 1155. Minority report on lands in severalty to Indians.

86. H. Ex. Doc. No. 247, 51st Cong., 1st Sess., at 71 (Mar. 6, 1890) (portion of Third Council at Red Lake, July 3, 1889).

87. Ibid., 82 (portions of final Seventh Council at Red Lake, July 6, 1889).

88. Ibid., 94-95.

89. Ibid., 95.

90. Moorehead, Warren King. The American Indian in the United States, Period 1850-1914. Andover MA: Andover Press, 1914, pp. 73, 75.

91. William W. Folwell, History of Minnesota, rev. ed. (St. Paul: Minnesota Historical Society, 1969), 4: 278-279.

92. Report of the Commissioner of Indian Affairs to the Secretary of the Interior, United States. Office of Indian Affairs, U.S. Government Printing Office, 1911, p. 42.

93. Report of the Commissioner of Indian Affairs to the Secretary of the Interior, United States. Office of Indian Affairs, U.S. Government Printing Office, 1912, p. 42.

94. Ibid., 43.

95. Youngbear-Tibbetts, Holly. "Without Due Process: The Alienation of

Individual Trust Allotments of the White Earth Anishinaabeg." American Indian Culture and Research Journal 15.2 (1991).

96. Peterson, Ken. "Ransom Powell and the Tragedy of White Earth." Minnesota History 63.3 (2012): 96.

97. Id.

98. Id.

99. Annual Report of the Department of the Interior (1891), Vol. 3, U.S. Government Printing Office, 1892, p. 375.

100. Annual Report of the Department of the Interior, Vol. 3, U.S. Government Printing Office, 1893, p. 401.

101. Annual Report of the Department of the Interior, Vol. 3, U.S. Government Printing Office, 1894, p. 464.

102. Ibid., 473.

103. The Legacy of Allotment on Contemporary Native Agriculture. Native Lands Advocacy Project. https://storymaps.arcgis.com/stories/c8397792476c4b8ea2f6f52b49ac6d7f? (accessed online September 27, 2023).

104. INDIAN LAND TENURE, ECONOMIC STATUS, AND POPULATION TRENDS, PART X OF THE REPORT ON LAND PLANNING, Office of Indian Affairs, United States Printing Office, 1935, p. 8.

105. Id.

106. Id.

107. Ibid., 9-10.

108. Ibid., 9.

109. Id.

110. Report of the Commissioner of Indian Affairs to the Secretary of the Interior, United States. Office of Indian Affairs. Blair & Rives, Printers. 1838, p. 17.

111. Report of the Commissioner of Indian Affairs, Office of Indian Affairs, United States. U.S. Government Printing Office, 1888, p. lxxxix.

112. The Abridgment: Containing the Annual Message of the President of the United States to the Two Houses of Congress with Reports of Departments and Selections from Accompanying Papers, Secretary of the Interior, U.S. Department of the Interior, U.S. Government Printing Office, 1892, p. 681.

113. Report of the Commissioner of Indian Affairs to the Secretary of the Interior, United States. Office of Indian Affairs, U.S. Government Printing Office, 1902, p. 31.

114. Report of the Commissioner of Indian Affairs, Office of Indian Affairs, United States. U.S. Government Printing Office, 1915, p. 62.

115. Report of the Commissioner of Indian Affairs, Office of Indian Affairs, United States. U.S. Government Printing Office, 1921, p. 25.

116. Report of the Commissioner of Indian Affairs, Office of Indian Affairs,

United States. U.S. Government Printing Office, 1900, p. 6.

117. https://www.digitalhistory.uh.edu/disp_textbook.cfm?smtID=3&psid=4029 (accessed online September 1, 2022).

118. https://www.loc.gov/item/2015657622/ (accessed online September 28, 2023).

119. Leland K. Wood, August 2009, When the Locomotive Puffs: Corporate Public Relations of the First Transcontinental Railroad Builders, 1863-69.

120. Schlebecker, John T. Whereby We Thrive: A History of American Farming, 1607–1972. Iowa State University Press, 1975: 141.

121. "Millions of Acres," Burlington & Missouri River Railroad Co., 1872. https://history.iowa.gov/history/education/educator-resources/primary-source-sets/changes-land-use/millions-acres (accessed online September 27, 2023).

122. Report of the Commissioner of Indian Affairs to the Secretary of the Interior. United States. Office of Indian Affairs. U.S. Government Printing Office, 1888, p. LXXXVIII.

123. Washinawatok, James. Recognizing an American Holocaust. http://nahmus. org/TOCscholarlyarticles.html#americanholocaust (accessed online April 23, 2022).

124. Annual Report of the Commissioner of Indian Affairs, United States. Office of Indian Affairs A.O.P. Nicholson, 1889, p. 3.

125. Report of the Commissioner of Indian Affairs to the Secretary of the Interior. United States. Office of Indian Affairs. U.S. Government Printing Office, 1890, pp. XXXVIII-XXXIX.

126. Ibid., viii.

127. Ibid., CLIX.

128. Ibid., CLXVII.

129. Ibid., CLXVIII.

130. Report of the Commissioner of Indian Affairs to the Secretary of the Interior, United States. Office of Indian Affairs, U.S. Government Printing Office, 1902.

131. Lewis Meriam, The Problems of Indian Administration (Baltimore: The Johns Hopkins Press, 1928.

132. https://www.doi.gov/priorities/strengthening-indian-country/federal-indian-boarding-school-initiative#:~:text=%E2%80%94%20 Secretary%20Deb%20Haaland&text=The%20purpose%20of%20federal%20 Indian,languages%2C%20religions%20and%20cultural%20beliefs (accessed online February 28, 2024).

133. House Report No. 443, 58-2, Serial 4578, p. 4.

134. https://www.archives.gov/research/native-americans/bia/termination (accessed online March 21, 2024).

135. https://www.justice.gov/archive/civil/cases/cobell/docs/txt/05012003_notice.txt (accessed online March 14, 2024).

136. Indian Land Consolidation Act: Capitol Hill Hearing Testimony on S. 1721 Before the House Resources Comm., 108th Cong. (2004) (statement of Ross Swimmer, Special Trustee for Am. Indians, U.S. Dep't of the Interior). Nash, Douglas R. and Burke, Cecelia E. (2006) "The Changing Landscape of Indian Estate Planning and Probate: The American Indian Probate Reform Act (AIPRA)," Seattle Journal for Social Justice: Vol. 5: Iss. 1, Article 15, p. 131. https://digitalcommons.law.seattleu.edu/sjsj/vol5/iss1/15 (accessed online March 15, 2024).

137. https://iltf.org/wp-content/uploads/2020/02/MR2_update_website.pdf (accessed online March 15, 2024).

138. S. 1721, a Bill to Amend the Indian Land Consolidation Act to Improve Provisions Relating to Probate of Trust and Restricted Land: Legislative Hearing Before the Committee on Resources, U.S. House of Representatives, One Hundred Eighth Congress, Second Session, Wednesday, June 23, 2004 United States. Congress. House. Committee on Resources, U.S. Government Printing Office, 2004 (accessed online March 22, 2024).

139. https://crsreports.congress.gov/product/pdf/R/R47908 (accessed online March 14, 2024).

140. General Services Administration, "2023 HISP CX Action Plan-Bureau of Indian Affairs," https://www.performance.gov/cx/dashboard/actionplans/2023/2023-hisp-action-plan-doi-bia.pdf (accessed online February 11, 2024).

141. https://www.governmentattic.org/43docs/DOItransBriefBiden_2020.pdf (accessed online March 14, 2024). In addition, the COVID-19 pandemic halted travel in order to protect the health and well-being of elders and others in the Indian community.

142. https://iltf.org/special-initiatives/estate-planning/ (accessed online March 14, 2024).

143. Interior's Fifteenth Status Report, Cobell v. Norton, Case No. 1:96CV01285, Judge Lamberth. https://www.justice.gov/archive/civil/cases/cobell/docs/pdf/11032003_notice.pdf (accessed online March 14, 2024).

144. https://www.performance.gov/cx/dashboard/actionplans/2023/2023-hisp-action-plan-doi-bia.pdf (accessed online March 14, 2024).

145. Nash, Douglas R. and Burke, Cecelia E. (2006) "The Changing Landscape of Indian Estate Planning and Probate: The American Indian Probate Reform Act (AIPRA)," Seattle Journal for Social Justice: Vol. 5: Iss. 1, Article 15, p. 134. https://digitalcommons.law.seattleu.edu/sjsj/vol5/iss1/15 (accessed online March 15, 2024).

146. AIPRA for Landowners, Indian Land Tenure Foundation's Institute for

Indian Estate Planning & Probate at Seattle University School of Law. https://iltf.org/wp- or-Landowners-Institute.pdf (accessed online March 14, 2024).

147. Nash, Douglas R. and Burke, Cecelia E. (2006) "The Changing Landscape of Indian Estate Planning and Probate: The American Indian Probate Reform Act (AIPRA)," Seattle Journal for Social Justice: Vol. 5: Iss. 1, Article 15, p. 134. https://digitalcommons.law.seattleu.edu/sjsj/vol5/iss1/15 (accessed online March 15, 2024).

148. Inheriting Indian Land Fact Sheets, Montana State University, Fact Sheet #14 -Definitions.

149. Jared Miller, Apr. 3, 2022, New Indian probate regulations create risks for pro se parties. https://www.indianprobatelawyer.com/blog (accessed online March 14, 2024).

150. Jared Miller, Apr. 3, 2023, Native Americans rarely represented by counsel in BIA probates. https://www.indianprobatelawyer.com/blog (accessed online March 14, 2024).

151. Stewards of Indigenous Resources Endowment, December 20, 2019, Comments on DOI-2019-0001, Updates to American Indian Probate Regulations.

152. Jared Miller, May 2, 2022, Getting a copy of the probate file is critical. https://www.indianprobatelawyer.com/blog (accessed online March 14, 2024).

153. Jared Miller, February 13, 2023, Another reason why Indian wills are worth considering. https://www.indianprobatelawyer.com/blog (accessed online March 14, 2024).

154. Jared Miller, Apr. 18, 2022, Why you should avoid appeals in federal Indian probate cases right now. https://www.indianprobatelawyer.com/blog (accessed online March 14, 2024).

155. Jared Miller, https://www.indianprobatelawyer.com/blog (accessed online March 14, 2024).

156. Vine Deloria, Jr., "The Indian Student Amid American Inconsistencies," The Schooling of Native America, Thomas Thompson, ed. (Washington D.C.: American Association of Colleges for Teacher Education, 1978), 25.

157. 2020 Report of School Districts, Chapter 8. https://www.cde.state.co.us/fedprograms/statereportcard (accessed online March 14, 2022).

158. https://www.law.cornell.edu/wex/order_to_show_cause (accessed online March 14, 2024).

159. https://www.indian.senate.gov/wp-content/uploads/upload/files/DoughNashtestimony.pdf (accessed online March 24, 2024).

160. https://www.thefreelibrary.com/Dealing+with+the+whip+end+of+someone+else%27s+crazy%3A+individual-based...-a0320732073 (accessed online March 14, 2024).

161. Miller, Jared, March 24, 2022, Estate planners must approach tribal trust

property with care. https://www.indianprobatelawyer.com/blog (accessed online March 14, 2024).

162. Miller, Jared, February 17, 2022, New Indian probate regulations target land fractionation. https://www.indianprobatelawyer.com/blog (accessed online March 14, 2024).

163. Miller, Jared, April 25, 2022, Even experienced probate attorneys can struggle in the federal forum. https://www.indianprobatelawyer.com/blog (accessed online March 14, 2024).

164. https://www.doi.gov/buybackprogram/landowners/wau-info (accessed online March 14, 2024).

165. https://indianz.com/News/2016/01/06/cobell121815.pdf (accessed online March 14, 2024).

166. https://www.ceousa.org/2020/02/26/percentage-of-births-to-unmarried-women/ (accessed online March 14, 2024). 2021 National Vital Statistics Reports, Vol. 72, No. 1, January 31, 2023 https://www.cdc.gov/nchs/data/nvsr/nvsr72/nvsr72-01.pdf (accessed online March 14, 2024).

167. DOI, "Indian Probate and Probate-Type Appeals," at https://www.doi.gov/oha/organization/ibia/Indian-Probate-andProbate-Type-Appeals#bullet1. (accessed online March 14, 2024). Hereinafter DOI, "Indian Probate." See also DOI, BIA, "Your Land, Your Decision What Is a Probate?" at https://www.bia.gov/bia/ots/dop/your-land#Q4. Hereinafter BIA, "Your Land." (accessed online March 14, 2024).

168. BIA, "Your Land." (accessed online March 14, 2024).

169. Id.

170. Nash, Douglas R. and Burke, Cecelia E. (2006) "The Changing Landscape of Indian Estate Planning and Probate: The American Indian Probate Reform Act (AIPRA)," Seattle Journal for Social Justice: Vol. 5: Iss. 1, Article 15, p. 167. https://digitalcommons.law.seattleu.edu/sjsj/vol5/iss1/15 (accessed online March 14, 2024).

171. https://www.bia.gov/bia/ots/dps (accessed online February 5, 2024).

172. Inheriting Indian Land Fact Sheets, Montana State University, Fact Sheet #10: Purchase options at probate.

173. Red Lake Indian Reservation, Minnesota, H.R. Rep. No. 183, 48th Cong., 1st Sess. (1884), pp. 1-2. Letter from the Secretary of the Interior, transmitting, in response to Senate Resolution of May 11, 1897 the report of Indian Inspector, J. George Wright, together with accompanying papers, relative to pine lands and pine timber on the Red Lake Reservation, in the State of Minnesota. (153 Pages of Testimony), S. Doc. No. 70, 55th Cong., 3rd Sess. (1899).

174. Letter from the Secretary of the Interior, transmitting, in response to Senate resolution of January 6, 1899, copies of letters and accompanying enclosures from the Commissioner of the General Land Office and the

Commissioner of Indian Affairs, relating to the estimating of timber and the cutting of dead and fallen timber on the Chippewa Indian Reservations in the State of Minnesota. S. Doc. No. 70, 55th Cong., 3rd Sess. (1899), p. 30.
175. Ibid., 32.
176. Miller, Jared, Jan 27, 2022, How to get notice of federal Indian probate hearings. https://www.indianprobatelawyer.com/blog (accessed online March 14, 2024).

www.ingramcontent.com/pod-product-compliance
Lightning Source LLC
Chambersburg PA
CBHW010113270326
41927CB00018B/3373